About the Author

Dr Michael Waters is a consultant, trainer, coach, author, conference speaker and, above all, an original thinker who has pioneered wholly new inter-disciplinary areas of study and practice. One of these, Surge Studies (www.surgestudies.org), was launched in **The Power of Surge** (2020). His most recent book, **Becoming Guise-Wise** (2022), argues for a commonality-first approach to relationships at every level as a way of increasing neighbourliness and ending conflict and division. Like **Should I, Shouldn't I?**, it provides a simple but searingly effective strategy for accomplishing the relevant objective.

Among his earlier books is **The Element Dictionary of Personal Development** (1996), the world's first general guide to the subject. Michael is known as "The Decision Doctor" (A name bestowed on him by a national newspaper). He brings his extensive experience as a decision-making coach and trainer to his latest book: **Should I, Shouldn't I?**

Michael is also a songwriter and scriptwriter and lives in Kent with his partner, Theresa.

Should I, Shouldn't I?

The best and easiest way
to make a big, scary decision

MICHAEL WATERS

Copyright © Michael Waters 2022

All rights reserved

The names of people in the book have been changed to protect their identities, but their stories are real.

While the author has made every effort to provide accurate internet addresses at the time of publication, the author does not assume any responsibility for errors or for changes that occur after publication. The author does not have any control over and does not assume any responsibility for author or third-party websites or their content.

flourish
publishing

www.flourish-publishing.com

To all the many people who have trusted me to help them make big and often life-changing decisions.

Without their involvement, this book might never have been possible.

Contents

Preface	1
Introduction	3
Chapter 1 • FOTS	9
Chapter 2 • Big, scary decisions: the background	29
Chapter 3 • Why we need to get decision-making *right*	37
Chapter 4 • Big, scary decisions: the reality	45
Chapter 5 • The best way	75
Chapter 6 • The Killer Question for helpers	121
Chapter 7 • Killer Questions in the public realm	133
Chapter 8 • A simple, crazy way to get conviction	141
Chapter 9 • Not completely convinced?	147
Notes	174

Preface

This is a deliberately short book. Here's why.

My experience is that people with a big decision to make, especially if they've been tortured trying to make it, want two things. First, they want clarity as soon as they can get it. They want to know how to make up their minds so that (at last) they can come to a definite decision. But they also want a bit of time to get to that decision, time to do the processing necessary and then finally feel convinced. They might not know at the outset that they want this time because they are understandably impatient to exit their ambivalence and frustration. But they nearly always do, because the way they've been trying to decide hasn't worked, so they need to understand why and find a way that does work.

I've tried to marry these two wants by making this book short enough to read in a very few sittings (so you can get what you need quickly) but long enough to walk you through the thinking that will lead you to know exactly what to do to make your difficult decision. This "working through" time also enables you to revise and review the kind of decision-making you've been used to doing, as well as for me to convince you that the method I am advancing will really work for you.

By the time you finish reading this book, I hope you'll feel confident and even excited to tackle big, scary decisions—and all other decisions—from this moment on.

MW

Introduction

Do you hate making big decisions?

Have you made some really bad ones in the past?

Does the advice you get from others often make things harder?

Do you need some simple ways to make scary decisions?

If you've answered yes to any of these questions, then this is the book for you. (If you've answered yes to all of them, then best read the whole of it now!!) What I'm going to do is show you where you're probably going wrong and tell you what you can do about it. The advice I give isn't going to be vague; I'll get down to real specifics, so that you'll know exactly what to do.

The great news is that the recipe I'm going to give you is,

in essence, simple. It's also just one main recipe that you can use time and again for just about any hard "Should I, Shouldn't I?" choice, or any other tough decision.

I'm also going to give you stories of what other people have done when they've had a big decision to make. Some of them did the opposite of what they should have done. Some of them did it in a way that minimised the anguish—it's these people you need to copy.

Making decisions is our existential burden; at least, that's one way to look at it. It's the price as well as the privilege we pay for being alive. Why? Because it's unavoidable. Why? First of all, because not making a decision is still a decision; deciding not to choose between this and that is still a choice. Second, because as long as we are alive we have to decide, moment by moment, where to place our attention. That's one of the most fundamental and inescapable requirements of existence. If you don't consciously decide where to place your attention—or you try not to—you are still making a decision. And if you try to opt out of that responsibility, then your mind (with a mind of its own), or something outside of you, will decide for you. It could be a social media platform, something else on your smartphone, television, an advertisement, another person or something in your environment. All you are doing is outsourcing decision-making, which is usually stupid and still a decision-making process, even if not entirely an intentional one.

If you hate the responsibility of making decisions, and having to live with the consequences, then you're not alone. By contrast, you may feel that you have a more nuanced view of making decisions. You might say: "It depends which decisions. I don't mind making some. Some are nice or even exciting to make." If this is how you think then you probably think that everyone else thinks like this.

But they don't. I've worked with some people for whom virtually all decisions are burdensome and effortful, even the ones that most of us like to make, such as which meal to have in a restaurant or where to go on holiday. I've worked with people who don't like making even the tiniest and seemingly inconsequential of decisions—whether to have a cup of tea, whether to wear trousers or a skirt. Having to make a big decision with real consequences can really freak them out.

When you lose faith in your ability to make a big decision that needs to be made, then that can make you feeble at making even the most trivial decisions. You just don't have the confidence. That's one potent reason for getting good at making the big ones.

Simplifying your life by consistently making the same decisions, so that you don't have to think afresh each time, can make sense. For example, always ordering an Americano coffee rather than battle with the welter of possibilities on offer. Or having the same meals on the same nights week after week so that it cuts out the need for drawing up a different plan each week. It's a life-management strategy that can serve you well. But using it has to be a choice. What's more than a tad disturbing is to come across individuals who have to make the same choices because they simply can't cope with ever making on-the-spot decisions.

I've worked with plenty of people who are what I call "you deciders" because whenever you ask them to make a really simple choice ("What would you like? Tea? Coffee?") they say, "you decide" "you choose for me" or "anything". It usually betrays a deep sense of self-mistrust, and beneath this, if you dig down deep enough, there's often a history of making big decisions with regrettable or calamitous consequences. Make a few of these, and you can end up nervous and alarmed about making the kinds of decisions that have to be made every day.

If this sounds a bit like you, don't worry. It can be rectified and, if this does sound like you, my objective is to change you from a nervous, "I don't like making decisions" type person to one who is confident about making them and knows how much more control over your life this will give you.

What constitutes a "big" decision? This is obviously subjective. What's big to you might be small to me. Is buying a new car a big decision? For those who take nine months to make up their mind (and many do) it clearly is. For those who trade in their old car for a new one without a lot of thought, it probably isn't. It's hard to quantify the "size" or magnitude of a decision. There will probably be a general consensus that the decision to get married is on the big side and the decision to have porridge for breakfast is on the small side, but try to find agreement about what determines "size" and you'll probably get a lot of different views. Is it about the perceived seriousness (whatever that is)? About the fear of getting it "wrong" (not so easy to determine as you might think)? About the possible unknown or impossible to calculate consequences? About the effort it takes to make? Usually all of these. But the kind of decision is also really important.

I was tempted to call this book: **Stopping, Starting, Picking, Parting.** I liked it as a title, but in the end I decided that it didn't make it clear enough what the book was about. What it does do is name what I've come to see as the four broad categories of decisions we find most hard to make (and keep!). There's some overlap between them. I'd be surprised if they didn't cover the kinds of decisions that have brought you to read this book.

What they have in common is that they are all imply some version of "Should I or Shouldn't I?" **Stopping** decisions include decisions about stopping bad habits, addictions and behaviours that aren't serving us, but cover anything we consider ending in our lives; **Starting** decisions are more or less the opposite of stopping ones, and include the decisions we make about changing our lives, ourselves and our behaviours (and, like stopping decisions, figure prominently in New Year's resolutions, personal development programmes and life spring-cleans!); **Picking** decisions cover all choice or selection decisions, from picking a partner to picking a toilet roll; **Parting** decisions include decisions we make about separating from a partner, a place, a job, possessions or even a gender definition or lifestyle.

Most of this book is about Stopping, Starting and Parting decisions, but I'm going to devote the next bit of space to Picking ones.

We can agonise over decisions of all kinds. Because there's often so much choice around nowadays, we can even agonise over which shampoo or loaf of bread to buy. It's not the kind of choice problem that over-bothered earlier generations or, sadly, is ever likely to bother millions of the world's poorest people. Picking problems are largely the province of the privileged and better-off. Choice is normally presented as a great thing, which in some ways it obviously is, but it comes with challenges, and I've known many people who equate "too much" choice with anxiety and stress.

This is not a book about broad choice decisions, where you have to choose one thing from a plethora of options. It's primarily a book about binary choices, stark and sometimes brutal and monumental, life-changing choices. But I am going to give you a choice-making strategy right here so you have one you can tuck away. After all, many of us need one, especially if we find choosing time-consuming and anxiety-producing at times. Then we can concentrate on the main focus: the strategy for making big scary decisions.

Chapter 1

FOTS

Some time back, I was shopping in Bluewater, a large shopping mall in the south-east of England. I'd been into a card shop to buy a Valentine's card, and right next to me was a lady doing something similar. I noticed that she had two cards, one in each hand, and her eyes were flicking between them deciding which to buy. I made my own choice and purchase and left the shop. I walked around the mall for ten minutes or so and happened to pass the card shop again. I glanced in. The woman I'd stood next to earlier was still there, her eyes still darting between the same two cards. What she needed, I thought, was a choice-making strategy that worked, a simple recipe for making a decision that she could make and move on from. That recipe is FOTS.

That lady was at the extreme end of a choice-making spectrum that many of us are on. Actually, not so extreme because she had at least narrowed it down to a couple of options. Some of us struggle to even get to that point. We get paralysed by having so many possibilities. Committing to one, and sticking with it, is a real challenge. So here's the simple answer: **FOTS**. It stands for: **First One That Satisfies.** That's the strategy I've come up with, use every day and find it works well. It isn't perfect but it's simple and applies to a myriad of choice situations. Its great virtue is that it stops you from going through every possible option. You go through the options until you get to one that satisfies. Then you go with that one. Simple.

What FOTS gives you is what the lady trying to choose a card lacked: a clear and specific **exit strategy.** An exit strategy is what you need to go from deliberation (i.e. considering the options) to making a definite choice. Without it you flounder. You don't know what it is that will make up your mind and determine your decision. You don't get closure, and staying open-minded can be more nightmarish than liberating. It's a bit like being stuck in a maze, going around and around, covering the same ground time and again and not knowing how to get out. The FOTS strategy has exit built in: you exit as soon as you come across the first option that seems good enough.

> Minds, like mouths, doors and legs,
> are meant to close as well as to open

For example: you want to book a package holiday somewhere in the Mediterranean. You want a decent adults-only hotel that is close to the sea, and you are clear about your budget. Instead of going to every possible website or getting hold of every relevant brochure, you pick one that offers a menu of possibilities and you go through that until you come across a holiday offer that satisfies your "look fors".

Then you book it. If that source doesn't offer you anything that satisfies, then you go to another one and go through that. You stop searching when you identify an offer that satisfies. It's that simple.

If you actually enjoy the whole business of looking for a suitable holiday package, and don't care how long it takes, then fine, don't use FOTS. Using it will curtail your enjoyment. If the whole holiday-searching process annoys and frustrates you then use FOTS. That's especially the case if you frequently spend lots of time searching and still don't come up with an option that really makes you ecstatic, or if you get really frustrated by your inability to choose between a couple or more of options. (Or someone else—a partner, perhaps—gets really frustrated by your frustration!)

But surely…

I hear the objections. "But if you do that, you might miss out on an even better option further down the line". Further in the holiday brochure. Further down the supermarket aisle. Further down the dating site profile list. Further away in time, i.e. some time at an indeterminate future point. You might regret deciding too snappily.

Yes, you might. That's the possible trade-off. But for one thing you will probably never know because you will never experience that encounter. If you use FOTS to make your holiday choice quickly and painlessly, and then look through all the holiday literature you ignored and find something more appealing, then you've only yourself to blame. You've given in to an urge that you should have had the strength of mind to resist. But you can't feel peeved or aggrieved at missing something you didn't know was there and probably never will know.

Using FOTS brings so many benefits

For another thing and this is the main point—opting for the First One That Satisfies cuts out all the agonising and everything that goes with it: wasted time, frustration, confusion, discomforting ambivalence, going around in circles and not coming to a definite decision. You can even feel that you're going mad trying to pick one option from a vast array of options if you insist on considering them all.

Think about the lady in the card shop. She clearly had two suitable cards in her hand. Either would have done her. If she had stopped searching at the first one that satisfied, she could have walked out of that shop contented. As it was, I'm not sure she walked out of it at all. For all I know, she could still be there, her head down and her eyes still flicking between two equally o.k. options.

Yes, you might say, but what if they weren't equally good? What if one option was better than the other? Surely it would be better to go for that option, even if it takes time and effort to do so, than to go for the First One That Satisfies.

No. Often not so. Apart from not knowing what you might have missed (so you can't miss it) there's the whole return on investment consideration. Most times the gains of considering all the other options beyond the First One That Satisfies aren't worth it. The gains are marginal. In the case of the card-choosing lady, one card might have been a tad more romantic or a tad more interesting, but was the time spent deliberating worth it? She might not actually have chosen the "tad more" card in the end. Why? Because when someone spends so long trying to choose, what can happen in the end is they panic and come up with a truly sub-optimal choice.

Avoiding panic choices

When someone procrastinates and ponders endlessly, they then tend to panic and that usually means a poor decision. The process sometimes goes like this. There's one voice in their head urging them to go for one particular option. That voice might be their own voice or the voice of someone familiar—their mum or a friend, perhaps. "She'd like that one", the voice advises. Then a second voice pipes up. "No. That other one is what I'd go for. It's more unusual." Those two voices go on debating with one another until you can't stand it any longer. A third voice—may be their own voice, maybe not—yells out in frustration: "For goodness sake, just choose any one!". This brings the misery-making indecision process to an abrupt conclusion. But the end result is a random choice made out of sheer exasperation. Chances are, they won't be happy with it.

Be honest, does this sound queasily like you on occasions?

If you agonise over making decisions when there are lots of choices, then this internal dialogue may be very familiar to you. It's certainly one I've teased out of many of the clients I have worked with. Sometimes, the arguing voices are both yours, but represent different parts of you, looking out for you in their own but, possibly, misguided ways. For example, there might be a cautious you and an adventurous you involved. The cautious you might say: "Go for that holiday option. You've been there before and you know it's safe and nice enough". The adventurous you might say: "Go for that other holiday. You've never been there or done anything like that before. Could be exciting." So you've got familiarity competing with novelty, the contraction or fear-driven impulse competing with the expansionist or possibility-driven one. That makes finding any option that satisfies challenging, let alone alighting on a suitable option quickly.

What can you do to make the FOTS strategy work for you? The best thing is to acknowledge that both voices have your interests at heart (you might even want to thank them) and see if you can somehow combine them at a higher level, as it were, so that they now seem like two sides of the same caring coin. So you might say to yourself: "I'm going to choose the first option that seems safely adventurous", or: "I want an option that takes me out of my comfort zone, but not too far out of it." Then the use of FOTS is back on track and you've the bonus of getting the competing parts of you working agreeably together. That offers the possibility of a satisfyingly optimal decision.

Look Fors: the good and the bad

Being clear about the "look fors" (the criteria) that are going to guide you to the right FOTS choice is one of the keys to contentment-making decision-making. It means you have already eliminated a lot of possible options so you have less choice to deal with. So, if you have "red" and "racy" as look fors when you're buying a new dress for an upcoming party, then you don't have to bother looking at all the dresses that are neither red nor racy.

But having definite look fors is not always a good thing. Sometimes the FOTS choice won't be one you thought you'd be looking for. That can be both pleasantly surprising and illuminating: it can tell you something about yourself that you didn't previously recognise. Being disappointed by the criteria you thought would guide you to an optimal choice isn't always disappointing. More of that later.

FOTS for anything! Really?

"O.K.", you might say, "I guess I could save myself a lot of time and discomfort if I use the FOTS approach for making minor choices that don't really matter. I see I could use it for food shopping, for deciding what to cook for dinner or even for more significant choices such as the weekend break option to go for. But surely it wouldn't work for really big choices, like which school to send my child to or which house to buy? If I used FOTS for decisions like these I would surely be reckless and I could come to regret it."

I'd say, maybe you'd regret just as much the choice you made through the long-winded, often exhausting and often frustrating process of considering all acceptable options. There's no good reason for not choosing a school, a house or a spouse through the FOTS strategy. All you need to do is promise yourself that you won't subsequently explore the options you never considered. If you do start to wonder, to speculate on the "what ifs?" then you know what the outcome could be: regret for something you can't do anything about. All that will do is make you miserable and undermine your continued commitment to the decision you made. It's pointless and self-sabotaging, unless it really isn't too late to revert to an option that now seems preferable.

"Yes", you might be tempted to say, "but what if we later come across a better option, a more appealing partner, for example, or a house we like even more?"

That's life. Live with it. You can't prevent encountering experiences however you go about making selection decisions. You can't stop yourself seeing other houses or other people who could theoretically be partners. Not unless you stay in permanent self-imposed lockdown with no media access. Besides, and this is a key point to understand, going for the first "satisfying" option isn't the same as settling for any old early-appearing option. Make sure the option floats your boat enough to commit to it with reasonable confidence and then get on with it. It's not foolproof and it doesn't guarantee permanent bliss, but it delivers pretty good results.

Perfectionism doesn't help

If you're a perfectionist, then FOTS is going to be hard for you to buy into, but it's exactly what you need. Perfectionists procrastinate and hold out for the ideal option that rarely shows up. If you're waiting for "The One", then be aware that you could be unaware that several decent "ones" might already have turned up; you just didn't recognise them.

You may know the story of the man whose house was flooded and surrounded by water so he climbed onto the roof hoping to be rescued. He had a strong faith so trusted that God would do that for him. After a while, a small boat came along and the crew offered him a lift to dry land. "No thanks", said the stranded man. "I'm waiting for God to rescue me". Shortly afterwards another boat appeared, and the same offer was made, along with the same response. And then a rescue helicopter appeared and again the man said: "No thanks, I'm waiting for God to rescue me". At which moment, a voice boomed out from the heavens: "For goodness sake! I've tried three times already!" The lesson: sometimes we don't see that our wish has already been granted. If we're a perfectionist, then that wish could be an option that's acceptable if not quite perfect.

If you recognise yourself here, then once you've understood that FOTS isn't about going for any old option that turns up, but one that liberates you from the agony of having to wait for the perfect one, then it can wean you gradually away from the miserable experiences you've almost certainly had with making big decisions. For choice-making, perfectionism is a curse. FOTS releases you from it.

Here's the thing: to employ the FOTS strategy is to acknowledge the reality of time horizons. From any particular point in time you can only "see" so much and so far. You can never see the whole territory (i.e. all the possible information you'd probably need to make an assuredly optimal decision) so you can't know if you are making the absolutely best possible choice. For that you'd need to know or see all the possibilities. That's often impossible and even if it's not, it's so, so effortful.

Imagine having to visit every semi-detached house for sale in Hampshire (or wherever) before you felt able to select the one you'd like to buy! What you gain from doing this kind of thing is rarely worth the effort. This applies to "big" decisions as well as small, inconsequential ones. And even if you did have all the possible information you'd need to make an optimal decision, you'd still need a strategy capable of making best use of all that information. Good luck with that one!

Not convinced? Still think the FOTS strategy sounds like settling for an o.k. option but possibly not the optimum or best one? Or just too simple or simple-minded?

Bear in mind that it's entirely up to you to decide what counts as satisfactory—what satisfies as "satisfies". There's a couple of things you can do to make it easier to know what satisfies.

Having look-fors is helpful—sometimes

The most obvious thing to do is to be clear about the criteria (the "look fors" I've mentioned) you have in mind and have to be met for the choice to count as satisfying. For example, if I'm shopping for a loaf of bread and there are dozens of different types, I know that "seeded" and "uncut" will be top of my list of "look fors". I'll almost certainly pick the first loaf that meets these criteria. Usually, the more specific the criteria the better. If you are searching for a potential partner on a dating website, then "no meat eater" might be more helpful to you than "healthy eater". If carnivores are not for you, then you can eliminate them very easily as non-satisfiers.

It's always a good idea to think about the criteria you will use when judging; it certainly makes elimination easier. For some choices, having clear criteria might be an absolute must. If you are choosing from a dating website and you have a faith that's extremely important to you, then it might be crucial for a potential partner to share that faith. I have to say, though, in my experience having over-fixed ideas about what you need your choice option to have or be can be unnecessarily restricting. Some degree of flexibility and open-mindedness is usually a good thing. You think you want X not Y, but you encounter a Y and it immediately grabs you. That grabbing is significant.

To insist on having explicit criteria and making choices slavishly against them is to over-rate the rational and the mental. In reality, that's not how we operate. We may well have criteria that are implicit and hidden, even to our conscious mind. They kick in, sometimes to our surprise, when they appear in an option menu. We didn't know that we were looking for someone from a big family, but now we've encountered someone who is, we realise that this is very appealing to us. We thought we'd only settle for a detached house, but we've come across a semi-detached one that we really like.

What are the lessons here?

- We often don't know what we want as well as we think we do.

- We often over- (or under-) estimate the importance of something to us.

- We can easily dismiss options which we come to realise are actually satisfying.

- An option we've never considered can suddenly seem acceptable or even attractive.

So deploying the FOTS strategy can increase our self-awareness—nearly always a good thing—provided we are open-minded and up for the occasional self-surprise experience, which can also be a good thing. The trick to try to pull off is to have look fors to narrow your search for the right choice, but not be so attached to them that you're unprepared to countenance other possibilities.

Also, as I indicate below, it's not just our conscious mind that's involved in letting you know when something satisfies. Combining the FOTS strategy with a spreadsheet of "must haves" and "must have nots" is rarely a recipe for happy decision-making. Uncompromisingly methodical decision-making doesn't usually end well, not even for the most anal-retentive of us! But spreadsheets and tick lists are comfort blankets for some of us, so I would never dismiss or proscribe them if I'm working with someone who cherishes them.

FOT Delights?

If you are concerned about the FOTS strategy not yielding you a good result, there's something else you can do. You can raise the satisfaction threshold by substituting "delights" for "satisfies". This will certainly up the stakes and will probably stop you from going for the first, "I suppose that will do" or the "just about o.k." option or the "I can't be bothered to look any more" option. It stops you from settling for something that barely satisfies. It moves the conviction dial from, say, 5 to 9. That is, you feel much more convinced by the choice you've made.

But here's the downside: if you've got to feel delighted or something even higher up the emotional scale (such as ecstatic) then you may not be getting the most obvious benefit of the FOTS strategy: all the time and effort it saves you, especially when the options seem virtually limitless. FOTS also cuts out the headache of having to decide which options to dismiss. You don't have to dismiss options you've never considered. In my experience, that's usually more a blessing than a curse.

Besides, it's hard to get delighted about many of the things we have to choose from—shelves of toothpaste, for example! Or even the profiles on a dating website, as long-time users will often tell you.

More important than feeling delighted is feeling reasonably convinced. If the choice satisfies then you should get a sensation the equivalent of "yes". This sensation more or less puts pay to the possibility of nagging doubts. So what you need if FOTS is to really work for you is self-awareness in the form of bodily intelligence. It's not the same for everyone, but chances are you will get some sensation in your gut or your heart, as well as your head, that tells you that this is a choice that satisfies. You could call it an instinct or intuition. Whatever you call it, it's one of the most crucial signalling sensations you have and you need to recognise it. Sensing or "reading" it will lead you to make much better choices because it's providing you with information distilled and gleaned from your whole body system and not just your head. It's tapping into the distributed intelligence of your brain, your nervous system, the "thinking" cells in your gut and the "mind" in your heart. And your gut and heart lie less, and often know more reliably what is best for you than your brain alone. Hence, the shortcomings of a spreadsheet or tick list approach.

Does it have to be FOTS or Nothing?

I recommend getting comfortable with FOTS in its purist form: that is, really going for the first one that satisfies. But you don't have to be quite this uncompromising. You can make use of the FOTS approach without being a total purist or applying it inflexibly. I use it in its pure form for most things, but sometimes I glance at a few options before electing for one of the (say) two or three that equally satisfy. I tend to use this modified FOTS strategy when there are so few options that there's no great effort in scanning some or all of them—such as when I decide which beer to buy in a bar. Most times the options are too few not too many!

I also use it when I know that I can look at a limited number of possibilities without being tempted to consider the whole field. I do this when choosing TV programmes. Generally, though, I keep to the letter of the law and really do go for the first option that satisfies. Since I started doing so more than twenty years ago, it's made life much easier and much less complicated, and I can count the regrets on half the fingers of one hand. It's also freed up so much more thinking space—unclogged what some psychologists and neurological experts would call my cognitive bandwidth.

It's like giving up smoking. Once you do, you don't have to spend half your time thinking about giving up smoking.

Making FOTS work

There's one more thing that helps FOTS work well. After you've made your choice, don't **look back** or over at the options you've turned down.

At first you'll find this hard, especially if it's habitual. It's just what some of us do. We buy a top, say, and then we give in to what amounts to a masochistic impulse to look at a load of other tops just to reassure ourselves that we've made a good choice or, insanely, to confirm that as usual we made a lousy one. It's just another one of the self-sabotaging and self-undermining strategies that some of us operate with. Learn to resist giving in to this impulse. And don't try to kid yourself that it will make you feel better. It almost certainly won't.

Instead, when you come to any fork in the road, choose your path and take it boldly. Put out of your mind the other path and what taking it might have offered you. In other words, indulge in no pointless "what ifs". But more than this. Commit to making your choice work. Going forward, do whatever it takes to stay focussed on your choice and to make it successful for you. That's where your energies need to go: not on finding reasons to regret what you've done but on giving your decision the best chance of proving itself a good one. It's the way of making satisfaction last.

Put another way: make **two decisions,** not one. First, decide the option to go for on the basis of the first (or, at least, one of the first) that satisfies. Then decide to commit fully to that decision and to making it a reality. This two-decision strategy is one of the golden secrets of effective decision-making. After all, it's easy to make a decision and sometimes just as easy to change your mind or not carry through with it. Changing your mind can be the right thing to do, but more often than not what's required is a commitment to implement your decision, come what may. It stops you wriggling out of New Year's resolutions and seeing them fall by the wayside soon after you have made them. It stops you backsliding. It stops you taking the coward's way out.

Deciding without committing can be worse than useless, yet it's what many of us do much of the time. It's debatable whether a decision not empowered by a commitment is even a fully-fledged decision. Anthony Robbins doesn't think it is. In **Notes From a Friend** he says that "A real decision means you have cut off any other possibility than the one you've decided to make reality"[1]. Now that's commitment! We'll be seeing later how to get this level of commitment in your own decision-making.

The advice I give my clients is to commit their decisions to paper in the form of written pledges. That makes them seem more serious and important—sacred, even. I also tell them to say these pledges out loud to themselves, not once but, certainly in the case of "significant" choices, time and again. So they might say something like:

This Golf is the first car I've seen that really satisfies me. My search is over. I'm now going to purchase it. **And then they do.**

You probably wouldn't want to bother doing this with minor, everyday choices, but if you were determined to make choice-making a discipline, then you might.

Keeping promises you make to yourself has multiple benefits, including gains in self-worth and integrity. It makes you a stronger, more courageous and self-assured person.

Using and following through with the FOTS strategy adds even more benefits. It builds your capacity to be decisive. Use it enough, and it increasingly stops indecision, which we could express as "in decision"—being in the process of deciding. Poor decision-makers dwell in this "in decision" space way longer than they need, and are still unproductive.

With FOTS you don't stay in decision-making mode for any longer than necessary. It may take some time to find an option that satisfies, but as soon as you find it you are no longer in decision-making mode. Being in that mode for a time is obviously necessary, otherwise all decisions would be spontaneous, random or, literally, thoughtless, but lingering in it unnecessarily can feel like being in limbo or purgatory.

When you start to decide decisively, because you know how to exit the deliberation stage, your mind-body notices how your behaviour has shifted. In effect, you observe yourself taking decisive action which "proves" that you are a decisive person. Your identity as well as your behaviour shifts in a positive direction. Psychologists call this process Self-Perception Theory. It's not so much, "I'm a decisive person so I make quick decisions", but rather, "I see myself taking quick decisions so that must mean I'm a decisive person."

There's always the risk that other people might see you as not deliberative enough because, unlike them, you are not poring over endless possibilities. They might think you are more reckless than bold, more hasty and precipitant than confidently decisive. My view? Let them. You've swapped the usually marginal gains of deliberating over all the options for the effort-saving device of going with the first option you are happy with. The benefits of that are considerable.

Actually, I'm pretty sure that people who criticise those I call FOTS users are quietly envious of them. They admire their strength of mind and decisiveness and wish they too had the courage to curtail endless rumination. As long as they are not completely gung-ho, "Go For It" people are nearly always impressive.

It has to be *your* FOTS

One note of caution. It should be obvious, but FOTS only works as intended when it's you using it, not someone else using it on your behalf (to put it generously, given that their motives may be less than wholesome!). I've suggested that FOTS can be used for major decisions as well as minor ones, such as which house to buy or which person to go for as a partner. But this does not apply if, say, your parents play a leading role in choosing a property or partner for you. That's not FOTS it's **FOTS*T*: First One That Satisfies *Them*.**

They may have your best interests at heart, but they are not you, may not share your explicit or implicit criteria and cannot experience conviction by proxy. They can't get your gut feeling vicariously. It's possible that you can agree with their choice, but it will be hit and miss. FOTS decisions cannot be reliably outsourced.

Of course, that doesn't mean we can't use FOTS for making choices that affect others. We do it all the time when we appoint other people to jobs or buy presents for them. I call this *Surrogate Choosing.* We make a choice with someone else in mind, but we are necessarily the choice-makers. People can't appoint themselves to jobs or buy their own presents, so we have to act on their behalf.

Sometimes it works well, if we have a strong sense of how they will perform or what they will appreciate. Sometimes it doesn't. We select the "wrong" person to be with or we buy someone a gift they'd never buy for themselves. But that's more about our judgement, or lack of it, than about the FOTS strategy itself. I use FOTS all the time for buying Christmas or birthday presents; it saves so much time and faff. I've also used it to make job appointments: not considering everyone who has applied for a job but a very small number and choosing the first or second person interviewed. In fact, shortlisting is a FOTS-friendly process, whittling down all the possible options to a tiny few.

In short, FOTS is short-hand for "Choose the First One That Satisfies **Me**". The "Me" is implied, although the "Me" can also be "Us" if it's a group decision. This is very different from letting other people decide for you. Be very wary of outsourcing the decisions that only you can take in your best interests.

Let's sum up

Use FOTS for any decision that involves selecting from a wide or limitless range of options. It will save time, effort and anguish. Remember: you don't necessarily make better decisions just because you've considered a host of options.

You don't need to be a complete purist. A modified FOTS strategy can also work well. If you think you will gain a lot from comparing a couple of options that satisfy without expending too much effort, then that's fine. What matters is that you get as swiftly as possible to a decision point without getting stuck down. Remember: the key thing is return on investment. The gain needs to be more than marginal to warrant the extra effort of considering multiple options.

It helps to know what you are looking for and the criteria that will guide your choice, but it's usually good to be open-minded and willing to entertain options you hadn't considered beforehand. Perfectionists: be wary of making a *look for* into a *have to*.

Once you've chosen the first one that satisfies, don't look back or reflect on the possible options you didn't consider. Remember, you can't miss what you haven't encountered or thought about. There are times when this rule can be broken, but reserve them for matters of real significance, and even then limit the time you give them.

It's fine to use FOTS for making choices that affect other people provided there is no mistaking whose criteria are being used (yours, of course).

FOTS is not for the weak-minded; it can be scary. As with all the best decision-making strategies for minimising the time, effort and anguish involved, it takes courage and a touch of ruthlessness.

Q. Want to choose more easily?

A. Then be more ruthless than tooth-less.

Using FOTS makes you stronger and more confident in your own judgement and judgement-making abilities. It's character-building.

Chapter 2

Big, scary decisions: the background

FOTS can be used to make big, scary decisions as well as all kinds of choice ones. As I've already suggested, you can use it to decide which house to buy (the first one you see that satisfies), which university to go to (the first one you visit that satisfies) or even who to marry (the first person who satisfies as a long-term partner). Most people don't, but you could and it might serve you well. I have.

But often FOTS won't be the most suitable strategy for the simple reason that many big, scary decisions aren't about choosing from a menu so much as choosing one thing rather than another. They are stark binary choices, usually some version of "Shall I or Shan't I?" or "Should I or Shouldn't I?" They can be excruciating dilemmas.

Although we live in an age in which fluid, non-binary identities are on the increase, binary phenomena are alive and doing surprisingly well. Binary is, of course, fundamental to computing. In part because of the internet and social media, our opinions and allegiances also seem increasingly binary (i.e. polarised). We are for or against something. Period. In theory, this simplistic, unsubtle, non-nuanced mode of thinking ought to make it easier for us to decide what to do when faced with what seems an either/or situation. But in reality, the hardest personal decisions for people remain the stark binary ones. We often use the term "stark choice" to describe them. Often, as we've already noted, they are fork-in-the-road choices: we have to opt for one road or the other. Often there's no in-between. If there is, or we try to construct one, then it is likely to be a very uncomfortable and unsatisfactory fudge.

That's not always the case. Sometimes the "stark choice" is less a problem to solve than one to dissolve. The "problem" either disappears or appears differently when we re-frame it or view it from a different perspective.

Here's an example. I once coached a head teacher who was wrestling with whether to stay in his job for another few years (until he was 65) or take early retirement. He still enjoyed being a head teacher, and was still doing a good job but felt he was running out of steam. We explored his situation more generally and the key fact to emerge was that he really enjoyed the little time he spent working with his wife doing hands-on work in her horticultural business. The conclusion we came to was that it wasn't necessarily a choice between remaining in a job that was draining or else retiring early. The third possibility was to remain in the job but with more energy and enthusiasm. How? By re-defining his relationship to the job. This head teacher got to the point where he felt he could build up his energy reserves best by spending more time doing horticultural work and giving less time and thought to the day job. He had no intention of treading water to retirement. He just wanted to find ways of being more smart and productive with his time in school, and reaping the benefits of doing more of what energised him most. We felt this seemed like a win-win decision for both him and the school, and he agreed to talk this through with his Chair of Governors.

Sometimes there are options other than those we've imagined; sometimes the possibilities are actually full-spectrum rather than binary. Sometimes.

I don't want to distract from the main point (that most big, scary decisions tend to be stark binary choices) but let's for a moment think about instances when that's not necessarily the case.

Getting into the habit of asking ourselves, "What are the options or possibilities here?" can be one of the best default responses we ever install in ourselves as our automatic response to problem situations. What often happens when we operate from this default is that we spot or generate a good many options. This helps us to feel liberated more than trapped, and to build resourcefulness. It's not easy to operate with a closed mind if we feel up against something. Being scared or anxious can make us blinkered. But if we require our brain to address the question of options, more often than not it suggests that we are not stuck with no choice or an either/or one.

For example, you might not have to stay in a job you don't like, or leave your employer. There may be other options available—negotiating a different role, for example, or a reduction in hours for you to explore other work possibilities. The head teacher I've just mentioned decided on an option that blended both these possibilities.

The same with staying or moving house. Modifying or improving the house you have, taking in a lodger if cost is the issue, letting your house for a while without surrendering it totally and living somewhere else—these are a few of the alternatives you have to staying or selling, depending on your exact circumstances. These are all fairly obvious options, but the point is, you might not always come up with even obvious options if you don't ask yourself whether there are any. I've worked with very smart people who have acted with a dumb mind when stuck in a situation they felt was a trap. They could only think "this or that" not "this **and** that" or "This or that or that" and so on.

And then there's **reframing:** defining a situation differently or from a different perspective.

I was once introduced to a young man who was struggling with the question: "Should I come out to my parents and the friends who don't know I'm gay?" Millions of young (and not so young) people have struggled with the same choice. I asked the young man whether it needed to be either disclose or don't disclose. He was puzzled. So I asked him whether there were other ways of defining the situation. He was very happy with his homosexuality so I asked him whether there really was a problem that needed to be wrestled with. "Couldn't you just live out your sexual orientation and let others come to their own, pretty obvious, conclusions?" I suggested. He responded very positively to this and, as far as I know, that's how he proceeded.

I confess that I am not an expert in "coming out" procedures and protocols and might have strayed from the advice given by those in the know. But the issue is not whether the thinking I elicited was consistent with current best practice but whether it was helpful in enabling the young man to see that his way of framing the situation was not the only possible way.

So often there are alternative ways of defining the situations about which decisions need to be made, and if we fail to appreciate this we might be stuck with either/or choices that are a long way from being the best ones.

Back to the central theme, which is that for the main part I'm going to focus on the "this-or-that-ness" of big, scary decisions because this is how most of us experience them. Here are some of the most typical "Should I, Shouldn't I?" decisions:

Should I stay with him or leave him?

Should I ask her to marry me or remain her girlfriend/boyfriend?

Should we start a family or not?

Should we adopt a child or not?

Should I go to university or find a job?

Should I stick with this job or leave it?

Should we stay in this house or look for another one?

Should I speak out or keep quiet?

Should I "come out" to my family or stay in the closet?

Should I seek gender reassignment or try to stay as I am?

Should I struggle on or seek to end it?

These tend to be the kinds of decisions we most agonise over. It's not surprising that some decisions scare us. A lot can hang on them. Our lives and our happiness levels are shaped by them. Make the "wrong" call, and our lives can be blighted.

Do you *really* know how you make decisions?

And yet here's the thing: very few of us are ever taught how to make really good decisions. Most of us don't even know what we are doing in our heads (or, more accurately, in our bodies and our heads) when we make decisions. Ask someone a seemingly simple question about what they are doing, and I bet they struggle to tell you. For example, ask them how they decide what to choose from a restaurant menu. Unless they choose the same thing every time, the chances are they won't know for sure. Ask them to tell you step-by-step precisely what they did inside themselves to reach a big decision (to ask for a divorce, say) and they will almost certainly tell you something vague, make it up or look completely flummoxed. They might be able to tell you some of the steps they took, but they almost certainly won't be able to tell you about the thoughts and actions that occurred inside themselves, and the precise sequence of those thoughts and actions, to come to the decision.

How many of us ever have the opportunity to find out precisely how we actually do make decisions and whether the ways we make them are really working for us? It's staggering when you think about it: the thing we do more than anything else, and often with life-changing consequences, is a process largely out of our conscious awareness!

Drawing out of individuals their decision-making strategies

(with their full cooperation, of course) is one of the most rewarding and potentially life-changing things I have the privilege of doing. Once someone knows or discovers precisely what they are doing inside themselves and, sometimes, outside themselves, to make a decision, then they can assess its effectiveness. They can begin to see if it has worked for them, if they are happy with it and what action to take if they aren't.

I've used the word "strategy" for the one way of making decisions (FOTS) that I've already discussed. We could substitute the word "recipe". I doubt you've ever thought about your ways of deciding things as strategies or recipes, if you've ever thought about them at all. And yet that's exactly what they are: strategies or recipes. The recipe for a cake tells you the ingredients to use, how much of them you'll need, and the sequence of steps you'll need to take to end up with the result you want—a particular kind of cake. Know it or not, that's the kind of thing you'll be doing when you make a significant decision. You may have different recipes for different kinds of decisions, but you can bet your life you'll be using the same recipes time and time again. And if they don't lead to good results, you'll be using wrong or unsatisfactory recipes time and again.

In the case of recipes for making decisions, the ingredients will be things such as scenes and objects you see, mental pictures, things you say to yourself (out loud or in your head) and certain kinds of feelings, which you'll go through in a particular sequence. The "amounts" or qualities of ingredients will be things such as: whether your mental images are coloured or black and white, clear or fuzzy, close-up or distant; whether the sounds in your head are voices, whether they are loud or soft, near or far away, of actual people or imagined ones; whether the feelings are emotions or bodily sensations, where they are located, whether they are pleasing or displeasing, and so on.

What you end up with when you "run" your recipes will be decisions you are happy or unhappy with, or maybe no definite decision, only confusion and ambivalence. Everything depends on how effective and fit-for-purpose your recipe is.

My intention in writing this book is to make decision-making part of your conscious awareness, so that you get an understanding of what you may be doing "wrong" and what you can do to put it right. I'm concentrating on the recipes you use for making big scary decisions but they may well apply to the decisions you make for all kinds of things. I'll focus on the main ingredients rather than on all the ways you might think about them in your head.

In NLP (Neuro-linguistic Programming) the qualities and quantities of the ingredients—things like colour, if we're thinking in visual modality, or volume in auditory modality—are called sub-modalities. By all means investigate this area further if it interests you, but we don't want to get lost in a mountain of detail, so I'll say no more here about the fine details of decision-making strategies. Besides, chances are you'll probably need a coach with the skills to elicit your decision-making recipes if you are ever going to "get them out" fully and precisely in order to scrutinise them.

Although I've developed my ideas from a range of disciplines, NLP included, I won't put these on show and I'll use as little technical language as possible. This is a practical book not an academic one.

Chapter 3

Why we need to get decision-making *right*

It's worth devoting a little more time to thinking about the importance of decision-making and, in effect, why I hope you'll be pleased to have this book in your hands. If you prefer to jump straight into the practical strategy for making big, scary decisions then go to the next chapter. But I think you'll find the following few pages worth the brief reading time you'll need to give them.

Decision-making is so pervasive that you can attach the phrase "decision-making" to almost anything you want and it will make sense. For example, you wouldn't be surprised to find books, magazine articles or their website equivalents with the following titles, and you'd probably be interested in reading most of them: **Decision-making and Relationships; Decision-making and Obesity; Decision-making and Shopping; Decision-making and Debt; Decision-making and Career Development; Decision-making and Forgiveness; Decision-making and Lying; Decision-making and Rape; Decision-making and Faith; Decision-making and**

Happiness; Decision-making and Success; Decision-making and Misery; Decision-making and Mental Health.

You could generate thousands of titles like these and they'd all make sense and seem to promise something of value. That just shows how important a process of decision-making is in regard to everything we experience.

Bad decision-making = Misery

I can almost guarantee that if we looked into some of the worst times of your life, we'd find bad decision-making lurking somewhere in the background. My work as the Decision Doctor, coaching others to make better decisions, has shown me how often misery can be ended by a decision and how happiness can be started by one. Or, even more commonly, how relieved and free people feel when they finally make a big decision having spent ages "in decision". And I've also detected a pattern: people who make bad decisions, ones that clearly don't serve their best interests and cause regret, tend to have a history of making them. People who make good decisions tend to have a record of generally good decisions. It's mainly down to the quality of the strategies or recipes they use to make them.

Interestingly, lots of people struggle to see for themselves just how much of their unhappiness or dissatisfaction is a direct result of poor decision-making. They think it's down to things that it isn't, such as bad luck or something in their past that only counselling or therapy can uncover and address. In fact, I'm pretty certain that many people are going through therapy to sort out their problems when what they really need is a better way of making decisions so that they don't go on creating the same problems. They certainly need a skilled helper, but it's not necessarily a psychotherapist or equivalent. They need someone to help them to understand the cause–effect relationships between their decision-making strategies and their lives and experiences, and then to help them to operate decision-making strategies that produce different and more desirable results. Here is an illuminating example of this.

Some years back I was training a group of head teachers on the theme of excellent decision-making. An important part of the course focussed on seeking to uncover the strategies (or recipes) those on the course used to make decisions, "uncover" because they were unlikely to know what these are. As I've said, they are so habitual and automatic we don't even know that we are using strategies. We think we're doing what just comes naturally.

One of the head teachers was eager for me to help her "pull out" her strategy or, at least, the one she most often depended on. She seemed to me to be a troubled soul. I asked her a lot of questions to help her identify the recipe she was using. It wasn't always easy for her to describe the ingredients and steps because they were so second-nature to her, but we got there in the end.

I had a good idea of at least one reason why she was having so much trouble making decisions that served her well: a clamour of voices in her head telling her different things. Her mum's voice was prominent. So was her husband's. Her own voice was not. When she had to decide something important, her mum's voice would suggest one thing and quite often her husband's voice would suggest something different. Often these voices would argue with each other. She would listen to them and too often either gave in to one of them or else end up confused and undecided.

On occasions, her own voice would tell her to "just choose" to stop the conflict in her head. Occasionally, her own voice would say something like: "For Heaven's sake, you're a grown woman, make up your own mind" and she would assert her own view, but often with no great confidence in it. This intelligent and, certainly to the outside world, successful woman, was lamentably poor at making personal decisions that served her well. She had a blinding realisation that so much of the dissatisfaction she felt about her life was a result of this and nothing much else. She spoke about a range of important decisions she'd made—about partners, going to university, going into teaching and later into headship—all using this unsatisfactory strategy.

This sad story gives the lie to the idea that all our decision-making processes are under our immediate and direct control, and that we know exactly what we are doing when we decide something. One of the reasons that decision-making can exert such a phenomenal influence in our lives is because so much of it happens outside of normal conscious awareness. That is, your non-conscious or unconscious mind makes decisions that you don't know about. It's probably behind your dreams, for example; you don't normally decide consciously what you are going to dream about. It's also responsible for some of the decisions that most profoundly affect your emotional lives. For example, if you grew up with warring parents, your unconscious mind might have decided that having a full-blown emotional life threatened your wellbeing. Years later, you may still be experiencing the effects of this decision; you can't express your emotions as you'd like, or you throw yourself into unloving relationships, and you don't know why. In this situation, a psychotherapist *could* be useful to you.

I've spent hundreds of hours helping to bring the out-of-conscious-awareness aspects of people's decision-making processes into their conscious awareness. It can be done (at least, to a degree) and it can make all the world of difference to some individuals.

Most of this book is about working on decision-making at a conscious level; the level at which we are aware that we are engaged in decision-making. The approach is "architectural"—consciously constructing approaches that work—rather than "archaeological": digging deep into our past experiences and our psyche to identify the factors responsible for our decision-making habits. The latter can be illuminating, but we'll leave that to the psychoanalysts.

This is not to deny the importance of automatic and unconscious mechanisms. These can have a major impact, and any time we feel that while one "part" of us wants one thing, another "part" wants something else, or that we are making self-sabotaging decisions—decisions which seem contrary to our best interests—then it is very possible that unconscious processes are at play. (A psychotherapist, or an NLP specialist in "parts reintegration" might be of help here.)

It's worth noting that it may be the case that virtually all decisions are made initially outside of conscious awareness. Recent neurological research seems to indicate that when we decide to, say, make a cup of tea, we are consciously registering an impulse of the will that occurred in the unconscious mind a second or two before.

A lot of cognitive specialists nowadays take a pretty dim view of the idea that we each have a will and it's through the conscious exercise of this that we make things happen. I prefer to work on the basis of the common sense supposition that we do will things to happen, and that we can make decisions with conscious intent if we choose to. I'll leave you to decide where you stand on this one—if your will lets you!!

What isn't in question is that decisions produce results. Decisions are important above all else because they create. And in the human world, not much gets created without a decision. Virtually every self-help guru in the universe insists that our destinies owe more to our decisions than to our conditions. Make and commit to the "right" choices, and you can get out of any set of negative circumstances and onto the path of being or achieving whatever you set your mind to. This is an overstatement and a simplification, but it undoubtedly has some truth to it.

Another way of putting this is to say that excellent decision-making is critical to effective *self-leadership.* Effective self-leadership is about being in control of our lives, taking us in the "right" directions (ones based on our highest values and most valued gifts, for example) and taking responsibility for the decisions we take and the actions and consequences which flow from them. And if we can't lead ourselves with purpose and confidence, then what chance have we of leading others satisfactorily (and those "others" might include our children and nearest and dearest as well as the people who work with and for us). Looked at in this light, doing everything you can to become an effective decision-maker is a moral and social responsibility.

It's not just the content or the **"what"** of decisions that is important. The **"how"** is also important, sometimes more so. Deciding without committing can be worse than useless, yet it's what many of us do much of the time. It's debatable whether a decision not empowered by a commitment is even a fully-fledged decision. As we noted earlier, Anthony

Robbins doesn't think it is. In **Notes from a Friend** he says that "A real decision means you have cut off any other possibility than the one you've decided to make reality". Now that's commitment! We'll be seeing later how to get this level of commitment in your own decision-making.

On the other hand, committing prematurely, making a decision based on too little information and too little awareness of the possible implications and consequences, when both sets of data are or could be available to you, is very unwise. One important aspect of what I call *Decision-Making Intelligence* is knowing when to be cautious about coming to a decision and how much caution to show.

There are other very important decision-making **hows,** including the speed at which we make and maybe attempt to un-make decisions. As we shall see later, excellent decision-makers tend to make decisions that can be made rapidly, and are disinclined to reverse them later. Not out of arrogance or stubbornness but because they've made them with conviction and a high degree of confidence. This is doubtless where you will want to be headed.

Chapter 4

Big, scary decisions: the reality

Emma and Greg were beginning to enjoy being a couple by themselves, at last. They loved their two children, but felt a sense of liberation when they moved out of the family home and started supporting themselves. Emma and Greg were comfortably off and enthusiastically making plans for the future, including early retirement and plenty of travel. Then something happened that threw all their plans in the air: Emma's mum was diagnosed with dementia. At first that meant that Emma had to spend more and more time at her mum's house caring for her. When that became even more demanding, Emma started to work part-time.

She and her husband then started to talk about whether they should bring Emma's mum to live with them. They spoke endlessly about it, and sometimes tetchily. They rehearsed the same arguments time and again. Greg focussed heavily on the cons: they'd be financially much worse off without Emma's contribution; it would take a big toll on Emma's health and wellbeing; it could have a negative impact on their own relationship; the kids would lose the spare bedroom to come back to for short visits. Emma had different arguments: she felt a duty to look after her mum; it would be more stressful to visit her mum every day and to leave her alone or in the hands of visiting care-workers for very short bits of the day than to have her at home; they could manage on just Greg's salary; postponing their travel plans wasn't a great hardship.

Emma and Greg drained themselves and damaged their relationship discussing the matter day after day and never coming to a firm or agreeable conclusion.

There are thousands of couples and families around the country in very similar situations having very similar discussions. They can seem insoluble, but they very rarely are. It's just a matter of knowing how, precisely, to bring interminable debates and arguments to a satisfactory end. That is, how to make a big, scary decision.

Sometimes the arguments are internal. They're ones we have with ourselves rather than with someone else (or with lots of other people). They can be equally if not more damaging and distressing. They can make us feel extremely lonely. If the American naturalist, poet and philosopher Henry Thoreau was right; that a great many people spend their lives in a state of "quiet desperation", then he may well have had the silently and chronically troubled decision-maker in mind.

Consider the remarkable case of Mary. When I worked with Mary she was in her early 70s and had been married to the same man for nearly 50 years. (For obvious reasons, I won't reveal his name.) I met Mary through one of her church-going friends who suggested to her that it might be worthwhile talking to me. When we met up she was, at first, hesitant and reluctant to open up about her dilemma, but finally revealed that she was unhappy in her marriage. Bit by bit she came to disclose that she was thinking about leaving her husband. I asked her how long she had been thinking about this. Her reply was gob-smacking: "Thirty years". I'd been used to coaching individuals who'd spent what they often described as "ages" trying to make up their minds, but I was truly shocked by this exceptional length of "in decision" time.

I asked Mary how often she thought about whether or not to leave her husband. I was expecting her to say, "every now and again" or "quite often" or "after we've had a row" or something to suggest significant intervals between the deliberations. Instead she said, and these are her exact words: "every day for thirty years". I asked her why she thought she still hadn't come to a firm decision after all this time. All she could say at this stage of our time together was: "I don't know. It isn't easy".

I'll return to Mary's story later, and to Emma and Greg's, but there are several features that they both share that will almost certainly be familiar to you if you are struggling with a big decision. First, there's the agonising. Second, there's the lack of progress: going over the same ground time and again and not getting anywhere. The two are related, of course. Doing a lot of thinking and talking that doesn't get converted into action is frustrating and stressful. You sense how wasteful it is. Third, there's the impact on the relationships involved.

Emma and Greg never fully fell out with one another, but there was a lot of irritability and bad feeling between them. This was not something they had experienced before. Mary kept all her musings to herself. She was aware that this harmed the relationship she had with herself, undermining her confidence and esteem and accumulating her frustration and sense of "quiet desperation". Not being open with her husband about the things she was considering may have kept them together at a physical level but it did nothing for their intimacy and relationship more generally. Mary told me that she was tense and snappy much of the time, as her husband, often mystified as to why, would point out.

As I'll show later on, I helped both Mary and the at-odds couple to get out of the maddening process of thinking endlessly and getting close to nowhere. The simple strategy was the same for both. It will be the same one for you. So let's spell out what we need that strategy to do:

- End your feelings of being conflicted and confused

- End unnecessary thinking and talking—unnecessary because it's getting you nowhere

- End feeling bogged down, drained, exasperated and overwhelmed

- End any bad feeling that's been developed between you and the other decision-maker(s)

- Enable you to exit the decision-making process and achieve closure

Let's condense this into a simple and positive goal:

My Goal for You

To give you a way of getting to the point of relative certainty from which you can make "Should I, Shouldn't I" and other difficult decisions confidently every time.

That's the goal, now here is a summary of the steps to get us there:

Step 1: The Essential Thing to Do First

Step 2: Avoiding the Worst Way (but 99% of us do it!")

Step 3: Understanding the Better Way

Step 4: Using the Best Way

Step 5: Testing You've Got It Right

So, why go through some not very good ways of making big scary decisions? Why not just go straight to the best way? That's a good question, and I'm pretty certain you'll see why as we go through the steps, but the short answer is (i) so that you can see clearly where you are probably having trouble being decisive and making up your mind, and (ii) because some aspects of the less good ways are necessary for the ideal strategy that we'll come to in Step 4.

Step 1: The Essential Thing to Do First

I suspect you've heard of the not very nice expression "going loopy". You may well have used it about yourself ("I think I'm going loopy") when what's going on in your head is driving you a little crazy. Where do you suppose the expression comes from? I don't know for certain, but it's a good bet that it's from going around and around in your head in an endless loop, not being able to change or exit your thoughts and not making any progress: that is, not coming to a decision and turning that into relevant action. The thinking you are doing when you feel "loopy" is wasteful and frustrating. It's getting you nowhere, except hot and bothered, so you might just as well not do it.

If you know what it's like for a vinyl record to be stuck on a turntable, then you have a good image for the idea of looping. And listening to a stuck record is very annoying.

I doubt there's a single human being who doesn't do loopy thinking. It's frightening how much of the same thinking we do every day, and probably don't even realise it. I've seen estimates of between 15,000 and 60,000 for the number of the same daily thoughts most of us entertain. That's incredible! Some of those repeated thoughts might be useful (remembering passwords and routes, for example) and some might be very pleasant, so we don't mind having them. But many of those thoughts will be futile and frustrating because they are the equivalent of bits of paper on your work desk: decisions that still have to be made. At their most extreme, they will be cyclically sickening or sickeningly cyclical. This is especially true of the same old obsessive thinking we can do in place of actually making a decision.

I've worked with many people whose lives have been blighted by loopy thinking and the psycho-emotional costs of it. There can be health costs as well. Keeping inside yet endlessly turning over thoughts that are eating you up can affect you badly. I've often been able to tell just from the appearance of someone that they have been chronically conflicted. And it's not only wellbeing that can suffer. Sometimes there are really major consequences for the person's career, finances or relationships.

So the first thing we must do to start making scary decisions as easily as possible is to **stop the loopy thinking.** And the first step to achieve that is:

Externalise: Get out whatever is playing on your mind.

How you do that is up to you; whatever feels right. You can write it down, talk to yourself or talk it out with someone you trust. But be careful with the last one. It's not just about trusting they will keep whatever you tell them to themselves, if that's what you want. It's also about trusting that they won't start steering your thinking in the direction that they think it should go. What you want is someone who can be a neutral, facilitating presence, someone who can be with you as you express whatever it is you keep thinking about, asking you questions to clarify your thinking perhaps, but going very easy on the opinion-giving. Actually, you even have to be careful about them "clarifying" your thinking, because even that can tilt it towards their way of making sense of your situation and that might not be your way.

Why externalise?

Lots of benefits come from expressing what is looping in your head.

The most obvious is that it can interrupt the looping. It may even stop it. Someone asking you questions won't allow you to go over the same things in the same old ways. Even if some of the content is the same the form of it won't be. Just the presence of another person will probably stop your habitual thinking patterns because you probably won't want to come across as someone who keeps repeating themselves.

If it's just you externalising—you are talking or writing to and for yourself—then you will almost certainly become more aware of the loop-like nature of your thinking. More than that, you will achieve some level of detachment. You'll be able to hear or see your thoughts as if you were someone else. That will ease the sense of being the victim of them or thinking you can't escape them. Your thoughts separate from you. That can be liberating and opens up the possibility of fresh thinking or new perspectives.

I've found that detachment and separation can be even more effective if you include physical separation. What I've often done with clients is have them write their decision-making thinking on a flip chart and then to step back from it. I've often joined that person—literally sat next to them some distance from the flip chart—so that we look at the externalised thinking together. I haven't necessarily said very much but somehow the physical togetherness has proven helpful; both supportive and reinforcing the idea that thoughts can be separated from the person having them and available for scrutiny by trusted others.

Externalisation is a necessary first step. It's usually necessary for the person doing it and it's certainly necessary for anyone trying to assist them. Unless they get it out, you can't know what their thinking is and, more importantly, you don't know how they are doing it. It's nearly always revealing and nearly always betrays why the person with the decision to make isn't getting very far.

It usually reveals that the person concerned is using the worst way of doing it.

Step 2: The Worst Way (but 99% of us use it!)

There are some very obviously dumb ways of making big decisions. **Randomly,** for example. You have to be mightily lucky for it to work out well. Choose a partner using "eenie meenie miney mo" and the odds on a happy relationship aren't great. It doesn't always stop us doing it, though. I've worked with plenty of people who've chosen their partners, their houses and their careers on a whim, or come perilously close to doing so.

Making big decisions when you are **in no fit state** to make them is also dumb, unless you have no choice. Doing it when you are mega stressed or depressed is asking for trouble. We've all done it and we've all suffered the consequences.

I've known plenty of people whose big decision included whether or not to have a really difficult conversation with someone. It was sometimes about ending a relationship, ("I'm really unhappy and I don't love you anymore"), sometimes about divulging something else of significance ("I'm thinking about packing up university"), sometimes about unsatisfactory performance or conduct in a work context ("Your behaviour towards your colleagues is unacceptable"). As I often tell people:

> The right conversation in the wrong state
> is the wrong conversation.
> You're not going to come across as you want to.

There's a third generally dumb way of making very personal big decisions: **outsourcing**. That is, giving somebody else the responsibility of deciding for you. It's the cop-out of the coward. I've known plenty of people outsource or delegate, either overtly ("You decide"), which at least is honest, or surreptitiously, where they've manipulated the situation so as to force the other person to come to a decision. I've seen it in work situations where, rather than tackle an employee who is deemed unsatisfactory or surplus to requirements, the employer makes that person's life so difficult that they make their own decision to leave. I've also witnessed it in relationships where one party conspires to behave so unreasonably that the other feels compelled to withdraw or separate.

That's all very sneaky and for me, at least, morally unacceptable. But it can also be bad decision making, even when it's in the open, if the person you are entrusting with your decision doesn't really know as well as you should what is in your best interests. Some forms of arranged marriage might be examples of this. If you are a supporter of such arrangements, then you might argue that parents can be wiser than their offspring, that they really do have a better sense of what will be in their child's best long-term interests. My contention would be that while older adults might play a part in the matchmaking process (introducing without obligation, for instance, or having some say in shortlisting for potential partners), the adults directly concerned ought to take final responsibility for understanding what is in their own best interests. That is, become more self-aware and judge for themselves on the basis of what they know about themselves.

Random, stress- or depression-fuelled decision-making are clearly strategies to be avoided. So, for the most part, is decision outsourcing, though there are obvious circumstances in which it is necessary, such as when doctors have to make decisions for unconscious patients and there are no family members to have their say.

The general principle is: be very wary of surrendering your decision-making wholly to "experts". If you trust them, then use their contributions to help you decide. But often they do not know best or value your best interests above their own. They may well have their own agendas: making money out of you, for example, or even using you as a guinea-pig for some self-glorifying experiment. Nowadays, even the best oncologists won't normally seek to decide treatment regimes for you if you present with cancer—commit you hurriedly to chemotherapy, for example. They may advise you and work with you to decide what's best, but that's collaboration not outsourcing.

It is easy to succumb to any of these three dumb ways of deciding—randomly, when in no fit state or outsourcing—when we are in a bad place (exhausted, bewildered or desperate, for example) and lack both savvy good judgement and a sense of agency, but at least we usually know we shouldn't.

The above strategies are recognisably sub-optimal. But there's a decision-making process that is also sub-optimal but that virtually all of us use because it seems so obviously fit-for-purpose. Indeed, it probably just seems like the common sense thing to do, perhaps the only thing that can be done. What is it?

It's listing the pros and cons, the arguments for and the arguments against whatever it is we are trying to decide.

Why the Balance Method is inherently faulty

I and others call this the **balance method** because the dominant image for it is a pair of scales or a see-saw[2]. I'm going to explain why this is the worst way of deciding. (Strictly speaking, it's not the worst way because deciding randomly or arbitrarily is way more stupid and risky, but the balance method is the go-to strategy for most of us, so it's realistically the worst way).

On the face of it, the balance method seems the obvious strategy of choice for rational people. There are always pros and cons otherwise we wouldn't be struggling to make our mind up. The decision would be bleedin' obvious, a no-brainer. You don't need to decide whether or not to eat screws and bolts for dinner or whether to marry your sister. Most people don't need to list the pros and cons for swimming in a polluted river or accepting a pay rise. For some things there just aren't any lists of pros or any lists of cons to consider. But if the situation has any complexity and looks anything like a force-field then there is a range of things to ponder. That's when it seems obvious and logical to (i) **identify,** then (ii) **list** and then (iii) **consider** the pros and cons in the hope that this will lead you to the "right" or the compelling conclusion, i.e. to your decision.

Sometimes it's not just our brains we enlist with the balance method. It can be our body as well, as when we imply that we aren't just thinking about the pros and cons but actually weighing them in our hands to get a tangible sense of their significance. We say: "On the one hand… On the other hand…" So we could call the balance method the **weighing method** if we don't just list the arguments but attribute some degree of significance ("weight") to each one.

But here's the thing: so often the balance method doesn't live up to its promise. It doesn't yield the logical outcome that the logic of the process would suggest. We don't end up confident, convinced and committed to the decision we've made. Often we don't end up with any clear decision. Worse still, having gone through the process—maybe time and time again—we can end up more confused and uncertain than when we started.

Recall the story of Mary. She'd done the listing of pros and cons on an almost daily basis for three decades, and where did it get her? Nowhere. As undecided as she was thirty years before. The same with Emma and Greg trying to decide what was best for Emma's elderly mum. They swapped pros and cons, did the weighing between the two of them and not just internally like Mary, so that they were struggling with each other rather than just within themselves. Different situation but same result: stalemate and no compelling decision. All very unsatisfactory.

It might be argued that it was the individuals at fault, not the method. Mary was just too diffident and afraid of coming to a momentous decision with life-altering consequences. Emma and Greg didn't give sufficient thought and weight to each other's arguments; they were stuck in their own positions.

These folk didn't refer, let alone defer, to other people (except possibly me) but some individuals do, and the result can be that the muddled become even more muddled. Listening to the views of others, especially if they are mixed (i.e. different others having different views) and even if they are well-intentioned, can make deciding even more difficult. And what if virtually every other person says you should stay but your strongest instinct is to leave (or vice versa)? This just adds self-doubt to the mix.

There's definitely some truth to the argument that the failure to decide resides in us rather than our method. Some of us probably find that we have more successful outcomes using the balance method than others. We might be more dispassionate. We might be more detached from preferred outcomes, less emotionally invested and more willing to allow the conclusion to emerge from a spreadsheet-type ticking process. We might be generally more decisive or more impatient, unwilling to spend more time on the process than absolutely necessary. We might trust our own instincts and judgements more than those who offer us theirs. All of this might be the case, but there is still something inherently and structurally faulty with the balance method. However well we use it, it is still fundamentally flawed, and most of us get floored when we use it to try to make a big, scary decision.

The flaw should be obvious from the images on the following page (see The Balance Method).

The Balance Method

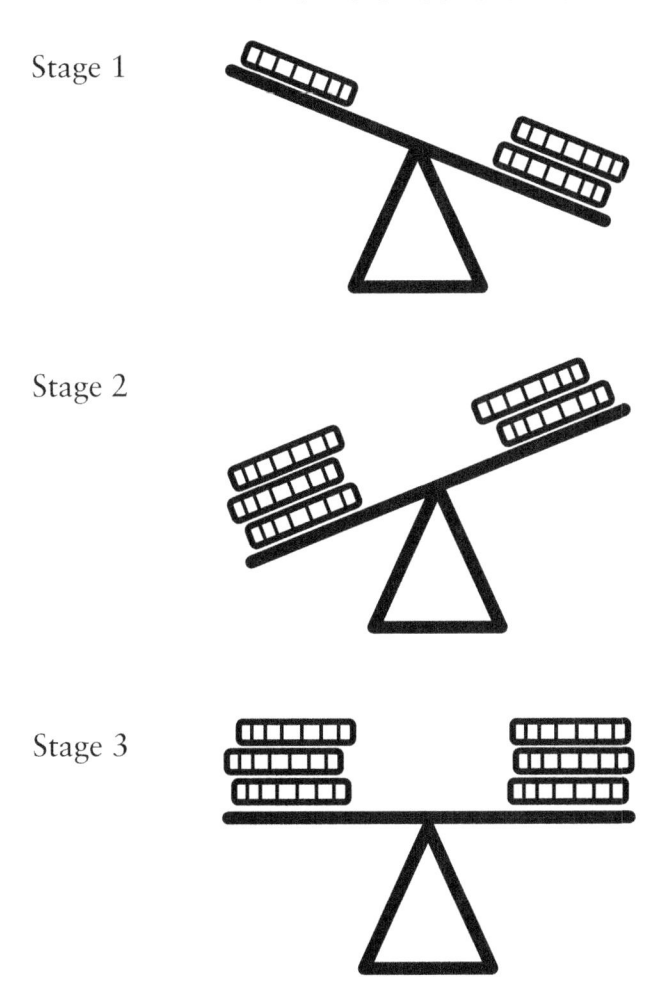

Stage 1

Stage 2

Stage 3

As we've noted, the dominant image for the pros and cons approach is a balance—a pair of scales or a see-saw. That's what's shown in the three images above. They map the deliberation process in a very simple form. In reality there could be scores of images and stages, with as much regression as progression.

It doesn't take a genius to see the flaw. You start by identifying and listing the pros and cons and think of them like weights on a see-saw. The first image shows your initial thinking: two of one (say, the cons) and one of the other (the pros), so the balance tips in favour of the cons. But, heh! You then think of a couple more pros. That tips the see-saw the other way. You could go on doing the same thing endlessly, finding more cons to outweigh the pros and more pros to outweigh the cons. This does not help you make a definite decision.

Neither does having the same number of pros and cons as in the third image. That's just stasis or stalemate.

You can see the problem. You can keep on finding new pro points to balance or outweigh the con points and vice versa. That means you just keep see-sawing. Even if you don't come up with new reasons for tilting one way or the other, you can keep on adding and taking away those you have already identified. That means the arm of your see-saw is never firmly and emphatically tipped one way or the other. The arm doesn't point to what your decision should be. In other words, the fundamental flaw with the weighing method is that ambivalence, uncertainty and disequilibrium are factored in to the very process. Feeling uncertain and not being able to make your mind up is almost inevitable. Exiting the weighing process can be perpetually postponed.

Listing can make things worse because the list can grow incrementally and indefinitely. You might think you've exhausted the arguments and finally come to a point of rest (the see-saw arm still and pointing securely down on one side of the debate) and then another opposing argument comes into your head and the arm begins to move again.

There's another unhelpful possibility: you find that you end up with (say) significantly more pros than cons but you are still not convinced that your decision should come down on the pro side. In other words, numbers alone don't turn out to be psychologically compelling.

Does all this sound familiar?

It certainly did to Mary, to Emma and Greg, and to scores of other people I've worked with on difficult decisions. In actual fact, the key issue is not about difficult decisions so much as difficult to come to decisions. I sometimes contend, contentiously, that no decision is difficult if you make it in the right way—by a process that's fit for purpose and without looking back. For me, that's highly encouraging, but I also know it's hard to stomach, so I won't push it too far. Not yet, anyway!

Joanne's decision-making turmoil

Someone who found that out for herself, after some conversations with me, was Joanne. Like Mary, Emma and Greg, she was in a quandary. She was (and is) an intelligent and capable woman, but she was in an abusive relationship with a man she adored. For much of the time, Joanne's partner was charming if more than a little controlling. But there were times when he completely lost it and would physically abuse both Joanne and her two young children. He could also be emotionally abusive.

Joanne had spent several months trying to decide whether to tell her partner to leave (she owned the house they shared). She had another decision to make: whether to tell her parents about the abuse, since she had said nothing to them about it. She knew it would anger and upset them but that they would do all they could to support her.

What was particularly noticeable about Joanne's deliberations was how contorted they were. That made her struggle twice as hard. Mary mainly battled with the arguments; Joanne battled big time with herself as well; battled with her ultimately painful and unhelpful attempts to minimise and deny what she knew was the truth.

By the way, it can be infuriating to listen to someone like Joanne who argues against their own arguments. Joanne had no problems articulating her reasons for staying with her boyfriend, but as soon as she mentioned the very valid reasons for leaving him, she'd try to talk herself out of them. Her problem wasn't just that she see-sawed but that she used artifice to try to stop the see-saw rocking at all. The trouble is, denial doesn't get you to the resting point of a satisfactory decision. If there's one good thing about the balance method it's that it usually represents an attempt to deliberate on the whole truth of the situation, not obscure key bits of it.

Step 3: Understanding the Better Way

The Balance Method doesn't provide a good way to make big decisions. The see-sawing is virtually unavoidable and can be perpetual. If you want a different image, then think of being stuck in a maze and constantly revisiting the same old paths: you're in an (information) field without a clear and certain way out. I'd be very surprised if all this doesn't ring true with you. Why? Because virtually all of us try to make big decisions this way and experience the same frustrations doing so.

So what does this tell us? Does it mean we are all stupid? Does it mean that we never learn from our experiences? Possibly, but actually I think it suggests something more positive. It suggests that most of us want to make an honest attempt to lay out the whole situation in full rather than obscure or deny aspects of it. Many of us inhabit echo chambers in our virtual lives where we only encounter opinions that we agree with, but in our real-world lives we are still willing to confront the whole truth of a situation. It may not be comfortable and we may need other people to open our eyes to some unpleasant truths, but at least we want our deliberations to take "both sides" into account. We sense that this is just the sensible thing to do because the truth is in the whole, not in just in a part of the whole.

By the way, the truth is not destined to be "in the middle", as some old adages and some people will tell you.

The instinct to represent both or all sides of a situation is indeed a good one and suggests that while the balance method might not lead us confidently to a decision it still has value. Indeed, it's probably a necessary part of the process—necessary but not sufficient.

Improving the Balance Method

One way of making it of greater value is to **add weighting to weighing.** In effect, that means acknowledging that some factors deserve more weight (or importance) than others. This addresses the crudeness of going on numbers alone. Just because there are five pros and three cons doesn't necessarily mean that the decision should go with the pros. The three con arguments might be far more persuasive, matter more and have more significant consequences.

If we stop assuming that all reasons weigh the same we move from having lists to having prioritised lists. This is what makes the weighting method a better one.

The tool to use for this is simple: weighting (judgement of importance) + scoring. Once you've come up with the pros and cons, decide their relative importance and indicate that with a score for each one. For simplicity sake, you could use either a 3 or 5 point scale, where 1 means not important for you and 3 or 5 means very important. You could have a range up to 10 if you prefer the scope it offers. I do. This has to be a largely subjective process because ultimately it's about its importance to and for **you**. Someone else might feel differently, give weight to things that don't bother you much and vice versa.

This doesn't mean that you shouldn't use other people to help you judge relative importance. Sometimes someone else can notice things that you don't. But they do need to be as dispassionate as possible and working for your best interests.

Consider the weighting Joanne attempted. Joanne began by saying that when her partner was sarcastic with her or her children, that was o.k., hardly worth a score of 1. It was his violence she hated. But what her best friend noticed, and I did too, was that every time she referred to her boyfriend's sarcastic comments she put her arm around her elder son's neck and pulled him protectively towards her. And when she gave examples of the sarcasm directed at her, she pulled her own shoulders and chest in. What we pointed out to Joanne was that she seemed to flinch and produce protective gestures when she spoke about sarcasm so this probably did quite matter to her. Joanne was a touch surprised but accepted that we probably noticed something significant so reassessed her score and now assigned it a 2.

A specific question that a coach or a friend can ask someone trying to work out the comparative significance of a factor is: "Does X matter more or less to you than Y", Y being a factor they have already scored. For example:

Do his sarcastic comments to you and the children matter more to you than his swearing, which he knows you don't like?

Or to give an example from a different issue (nothing to do with Joanne):

Does the salary you get from your current job matter more to you than the fact that you work with people you like?

If you are the coaching friend, then you may sometimes need to encourage your friend to dig deep in themselves and be as honest with themselves as they can be.

An alternative and sometimes more helpful formulation is:

If you could get rid of either X or Y, which would it be?

Sometimes, the following version of the question works even better:

If you could have only X or Y, then which would you go for? For example:

If you could have either a good salary, like the one you've got, or workmates you got on well with, which would it be? (Assume you can't be confident of having both)

Being able to assess the relative importance of factors or reasons is not always easy, and sometimes way more difficult

65

than you might imagine it should be, so asking these kinds of questions can help the person concerned come to judgements. They can begin to work out a rank order of importance. This is really helpful.

Of course, you can address these questions to yourself if you want to help yourself to decide relative weightings.

Scoring Kinaesthetically

Sometimes we can find it hard to assign a number to a pro or con reason. It's a troubling intellectual calculation that doesn't always come easily or with conviction.

Is there another way of scoring, other than doing it in our head?

Yes. It's using our whole body and the intelligence within it. I call it the **kinaesthetic continuum for deciding.** That's a grand term for something simple.

What you do is imagine that there's a line on the floor of the room or space you are in. It stretches from 1 at one end (unimportant) to, say, 10 at the other (couldn't be more important). Better still, place on the floor along that imaginary line a series of, say, table mats or sheets of paper, to represent each of the numbers along the kinaesthetic continuum (as below).

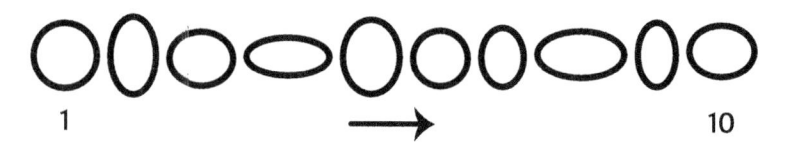

OOoOOoOO
1   →   10

Focus upon a pro or a con in the form of a question, such as: "How important to me is the salary I'm paid?" when you are trying to decide whether or not to leave your job.

Then walk along the line representing the reason's spectrum of importance and you stop at the point (or on the mat or paper) that feels right. You may be surprised at just how strong that feeling is. Step back and it probably won't feel right. Step forward and it probably won't feel right. Stop at the point your mind-body "tells" you to stop and that will be the score you give that reason.

You might start off with a possible score in your head; say, 5. When you walk the continuum you may find that you stop at a different score—say, 6 or 7—which again surprises you, but feels right. Or you might not be able to advance beyond 4. It suggests that you know deep inside how significant that pro or con is, even if your conscious mind indicates something different. If you feel 4 is the right place to stop it suggests that salary may be less important to you than you thought.

The technique is kinaesthetic because it involves both bodily movements and bodily sensations. You sense significance rather than try to work it out mentally. For some people, this technique works incredibly well. Not so well for others. It can throw up some surprising results and, therefore, insights.

I'll give you one example. I once coached a man who was already in a very well-paid job but was also keen to launch out on his own. His goal, he said, was to become as rich as possible, perhaps even a billionaire. I asked him to give a 1–10 score for how important becoming extremely rich was to him. He said 10. So I suggested he try the kinaesthetic continuum method of scoring.

The result was revealing and riveting. He got to 6 and stopped. He tried to go forward but felt, literally, riveted to the spot. I suggested three possibilities. Either he had way over-estimated the importance of wealth to him, which meant that there were other salient motivators at play, or else at some level he didn't really believe he ever could become mega-wealthy. Or, and I suspect this was the most likely possibility, it could mean that his mind-body sensed that being mega-wealthy might not bring the happiness the conscious mind imagined. It could have been all three.

He struggled with the outcome and what it signified, but it sent him back to the drawing board to formulate a goal that he could buy into fully.

To sum up: when trying to assign a weight, a level of importance, to a reason for or against taking a decision, there are two ways of doing so. Both involve a score chosen from a range of scores, from low (not important) to high (very important). The obvious method is to do it mentally—to think and reason your way to a number. The other way is to "walk it out" and trust that your mind-body system will tell you what the score should be.

If you are making a big, scary decision it makes sense to use both methods to be as clear and certain as you can be about how significant each of your arguments for and against really are. Personally, I'd try scoring in the standard way by thinking things through and adducing the evidence to support it, and then test it out kinaesthetically. Discrepant scores should make you review and revise. Again, speaking personally, I'd be inclined to give more credence to the kinaesthetic method, especially if you experience a strong pull to one score, especially if the decision involved something with a lot of associated emotion.

Let's return to Mary's story and her experience with weighting, which she did with a lot of going inside to sense and think her way to scores on a simple 1–3 scale. We later came to realise that the range could helpfully have been wider. A 1–3 scale didn't allow sufficient discrimination between factors of little importance and factors of great significance.

Below is a simplified list of Mary's reasons and the scores she gave them. Mary, you'll recall, was trapped in a daily struggle—almost a routine—of trying to decide whether to leave or stay with the man she had been married to for more than three decades.

Mary's Scores (a sample only)

Pros (for staying)

He pays the bills	1
He is a decent enough dad	1
He allows me a lot of freedom	2

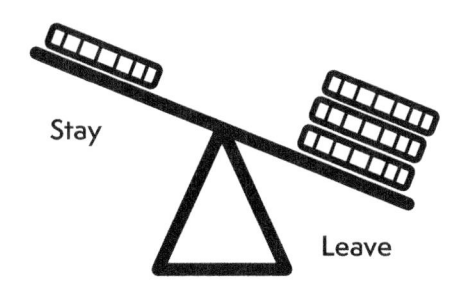

Cons (for leaving)

He's boring	2
He's tight	2
He isn't caring	3
I don't love him	3+

Mary identified many other reasons for either staying or leaving her husband, none of them more important than the two 3 scores (3+ in one case). She said she found the process of attaching scores to reasons useful and that she changed her mind about some of them just because she was impelled to really think about them.

What she ended up with was a shortlist of the really important factors that swayed her one way or the other and they too were in some form of priority order. That shortlist proved vitally helpful later on, but in itself it did not enable her to finally end her vacillation. When she totted up the scores for both sides of the argument they came to pretty much the same totals. They also had similar spreads—similar numbers of 1s, 2s and 3s. Mary said that she felt she was "moving in the right direction" but was still uncertain as to what she should do.

We tried a similar exercise, this time focussing specifically on the possible consequences of staying with or leaving her husband.

The Consequences

Pros (for staying)

    I might struggle financially   2
    I might feel lonely   1
    I will miss my home   2

Cons (for leaving)

    I'll have more freedom to find work I like   2
    I won't feel as lonely as I do now   3
    I might find someone who wants me   3+

This exercise also helped Mary to think things through and prioritise her reasons for staying or leaving. She sensed a preferred direction of travel (to leave) but again it didn't lead her to decisive action.

Much the same proved true of Emma and Greg's and of Joanne's weighting exercises. They all felt the process had given them greater clarity but still didn't lead them to decide with certainty and conviction the best course of action. In other words, they still couldn't make up their minds once and for all.

If you haven't done so already, try going through a similar process and see how helpful you find it. Focus on an issue where you are having a tug-of-war with yourself. Identify the pros and cons or, using this image, the pull factors in both directions. What makes you want to decide one way? What the other way?

The issue may be more complicated. For example, you might have a three-way pull issue, a triangular rather than a linear tug-of-war situation. That was really the situation with Emma's mum. Emma and Greg were wrestling with three options: support her in her own home, have her living with them, or "encourage" her to go into a care home. Where there are more than two possibilities, the dynamics are more complicated, but the process of scoring and prioritising is similar.

Once you've completed the exercise, by yourself or with the assistance of someone you trust to act in your best interests, see whether you feel more certain about the decision you should make. Chances are you will feel more certain but nowhere near 100% certain. You will still not get what you crave: a resounding "yes" response ("Yes, this is the right decision") from your mind, your gut and every other bit of your body.

Don't worry. The stages you've gone through have not been a waste of time. They have been preparatory. Identifying, weighing and weighting the arguments have laid the groundwork for what will finally get you to a confident decision. Could you have short-circuited them? Could you have gone straight to the "Best Way"? My experience is: yes, in theory, especially if you already have a strong idea of what your decision should be, but the preparatory stages are best not skipped. Deliberation helps you to sort out the wheat from the chaff. Rumination can give you insights you didn't have before and get you connecting to your values and instincts so that you better appreciate what matters and what doesn't. You'll be surprised at some of the scores you give—lower or higher than you would have previously thought.

Let's now move to Step 4, what I'm calling "The Best Way" to make a big, scary decision.

Chapter 5

The best way

We've established that nearly all of us make big decisions in the same basic way. At least we do if we are trying to do it seriously, thoughtfully and honestly. We've noted some of the other ways of doing so, including randomly and outsourcing to someone else, and agreed, I hope, that these are at best sub-optimal. If we try to decide rationally and with all the information available to us, then most of us will use what I've variously called the Balance Method, See-Sawing and Weighing and Weighting. These terms all amount to the same thing.

The image they imply is the balance or set of scales. This image can evoke a kitchen gadget (weighing ingredients for cooking) but it also evokes a court of law: the Scales of Justice on The Old Bailey in London, for instance. It's the court setting we're concerned with here, because when we use the balance method we are doing pretty much what judges and juries do in a court of law. They listen to all the evidence from the defence side and the prosecution side and try to weigh up the arguments made so as to decide which side to come down on. "Is this person guilty or not guilty?" is the equivalent of "Should I stay or go?" and all the other big, scary versions of this.

Juries and judges can have really big decisions to make. When there appears to be compelling arguments both for and against the guilt of the defendant, juries often agonise. Judges, too, presumably. Juries can spend days deliberating and still not come to a decision they hold with conviction. All this is much the same with most of us when we are trying to make a big decision.

What does this suggest? Something really important: best not approach difficult decision-making as if you were a judge or jury. At least, not in the final analysis; in the early stages, very possibly.

Diagnose your way to a decision

A more secure way of coming to a decision is through the process of **diagnosis.** This involves **applying tests** and **elimination.** Not weighing the evidence but filtering it. This is what doctors tend to do, so be more like a doctor than a judge or a jury. That's the best way of making a big decision.

If you visit your GP for a check-up, it is unlikely s/he'll take a pros and cons approach to the information you provide and the tests s/he does on you. S/he won't say:

On the one hand, you have pains in your chest and find it very hard to breathe. On the other hand, your hearing is perfect, your bowel movements regular, your diet is excellent and you have no muscle pain, so on balance you're a healthy individual. Off you go.

That's not the kind of decision-making you want from a doctor. That's not what diagnosis should be all about.

What you expect a doctor to do is use the information s/he elicits from you together with the information provided by the tests s/he applies and puts you through to come to a diagnosis based not so much on balance of probability (though there might be an element of this) so much as elimination: i.e. ruling out certain possibilities to arrive at the most likely conclusion.

The image for this is something like a reverse filtration system, not a pair of scales. Imagine a vertically arranged set of filters (or sieves) each one taking out the least significant or relevant bits of information until what remains leads to an almost certain diagnostic decision. Filtering usually takes out the biggest elements first; that's why I'm calling this the reverse model. What you end up with are the most telling elements (see below).

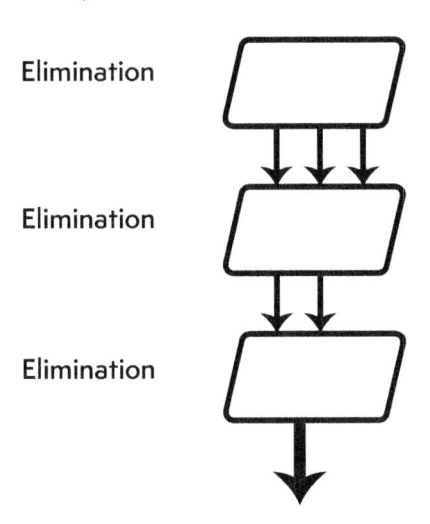

Elimination

Elimination

Elimination

Diagnosis: Decision

I'm going to work with the image of the filters, but the image of a drill—drilling down to the core or heart of the issue—would also work well.

Here's how a doctor might use elimination to "filter" his or her way to a decision about a patient's condition.

Q. Does this patient have a high temperature?

A. Yes? Then it's unlikely to be (a) or (c) but it could be (b), (d), or (e).

Q. Does he have a rash?

A. Yes? Then it won't be (d) but it could be (b) or (e).

Q. Does the rash disappear when pressed with a glass?

A. Yes? Then it won't be (c) and so is almost certainly (b).

Conclusion: The patient has condition (b).

The conditions medics seem to find most hard to identify accurately—currently, for example, Lyme disease and sepsis—are those where elimination is more challenging because many of the symptoms are common to various other conditions. The process doesn't reach the final filters, as it were, because there are too few tests or indicators to filter out all the other possibilities. I'm not a medical doctor, but I think I've got this right.

I'm not suggesting that this is precisely how medical doctors diagnose patients and come to a decision about their condition. They may not use an obvious Question/Answer format. Experienced doctors may use shortcuts, heuristics and typical symptom patterns based on what they've seen many times before to make rapid judgements. But elimination thinking will almost certainly be central to their decision-making. Some symptoms will shout louder than others, will be more telling, more salient and more reliable indicators of the person's condition.

A patient may have a dozen symptoms but only three are truly tell-tale. For diagnostic purposes, deciding what's wrong with the patient as a basis for treating them, the other nine symptoms carry very little weight. They might even be regarded as "noise" in the technical communications sense of unwanted information. The focus needs to be on identifying the crucial "critical few". It's these that give the game away. These are the "clincher" symptoms because they leave no doubt about what the decision has to be.

When Covid-19 was rampant in 2020, the three most give-away symptoms were a high temperature, a chronic cough and a loss of taste and smell. These were the critical few, though they weren't all present in all those infected and there was a range of other less indicative symptoms.

The Big Secret of Confident Decision-Making

So now you know what it is. It is: **think more like a doctor than a judge.** To make your decision, (i) eliminate anything that doesn't seem pertinent or significant, and (ii) use TESTS more than REASONS, or turn reasons (pros and cons) into tests. Formulate tests as questions or conditions.

Let's consider an example of the latter: the translation process of turning REASONS into TESTS.

James (not his real name) was a top-class rugby player in his early 30s. He had sustained some nasty physical injuries during the course of his playing career, which other people knew about, but his main issue was anxiety and panic attacks, which almost no one apart from his girlfriend knew about. His anxiety issues were becoming more severe, and his girlfriend wanted him to come clean about them so that he could get professional help. She also thought he should think about retiring, because preparing for matches was taking its toll. James loved his job and was loathe to give it up.

He and his girlfriend regularly spoke about what he should decide. Hide, play down or reveal the extent of his mental health issues? Carry on playing or take early retirement? They made very little headway all the time they focussed on the reasons (the arguments for and against both lines of action). That changed when they turned some of the key reasons into tests, i.e. the conditions that had to be met.

For example:

I know I shouldn't, but I'll feel pathetic if people know I get panic attacks, so I don't want to say anything. (REASON)

Became:

I'll talk about my anxiety issues provided I don't have to mention the panic attacks. (TEST)

and

I'll only talk about my issues when I'm convinced I'll be able to come across as strong rather than feeble.

Rugby is all I know. (REASON)

Became:

When I find something else I really want to do, then I'll think seriously about retiring.

Some of James' tests would probably leave some people feeling a bit uneasy; the one here about keeping quiet about the panic attacks is an example. But they made it a lot easier for James to make progress in his decision-making and for him and his girlfriend to be more in agreement.

Switching from weighing pros and cons to identifying some conditional tests looks as if it should be reasonably straightforward, just a matter of tweaking the form of expression. In practice, some people find it quite a stretch, mainly I think because they have been so wedded to pros and cons thinking that translating reasons for or against into box-ticking equivalents is all a bit of a challenge—at least to begin with.

Challenging or not, it's a process that can completely change the decision-making process for the better. If you have to decide something big, then it's so much more efficient to set tests you can tick if they are met than pondering over the significance (if any) of the reasons you have for deciding one way or the other. It's the difference between ticking achieved items on a to-do list (taking steps forward) and juggling (endlessly circling). It's what helps doctors arrive at decisions about their patients' condition.

Of course, doctors and judges don't plough completely different furrows decision-making wise. Judges do some of the thinking that doctors do and doctors do some of the thinking that judges do, but the emphasis is different. Judges specialise in balance of probability thinking. Doctors specialise in testing and elimination thinking, filtering to get to the critical few that will indicate what the diagnostic decision needs to be. This is the best type of thinking for making big, scary decisions, so let's summarise what this involves.

- Shift your thinking from "what are the reasons for and against?" to "what tests should I set to make clear the conditions that need to be met for me to decide a particular way?" Call this "tick-box thinking" if that makes it seem more familiar to you.

- Eliminate anything that is not going to be a critical factor in your decision making. These things are noise and ultimately time-wasters.

- Focus attention on the few factors that will be critical to your decision-making. The ideal is to get to the "Critical One"—the one factor that will do more than anything else to swing you one way or another.

- Put your energy into fashioning this into a question with a "yes" or "no" answer, or something just as definite. This question needs to be a crucial test. It's vital not just that you ask the right question but that you formulate it as precisely as you can. This answer will do more than anything else to determine your decision.

Elimination: How to do it

Eliminate anything that won't sway you

If you did the kind of weighting and scoring exercise we did earlier, you will have ended up with a lot of low-score reasons. If you haven't, then you've almost certainly failed to discriminate well enough. **Very rarely is everything of equal significance. Some things always matter more.** So let's assume you have discriminated well and half of the reasons you came up with on either or both sides of the argument score 1. This tells you immediately that they weren't that important to you, and no amount of deliberation is likely to make them critical to your final decision. So dump them. They're not worth bothering with and will only get in the way of your seeing a clear path forward. They are noise or clutter, and once you see them like that you see one of the reasons why the balance method is so unsatisfactory: because you've bogged yourself down in a lot of unnecessary, lead-nowhere consideration.

What Mary eliminated

You'll recall that two of Mary's reasons for staying with her husband was that he paid the bills and was a good dad. But she only gave them a score of 1. When we talked about these it was obvious that neither had any significant weighting or "swaying power". Mary knew that these things would have no bearing on her final decision; she was never going to decide to stay with him on the basis of these things. Being a good dad might have been a 2 or higher when the children were younger, but they were now close to middle age.

We shed all the other 1 scoring reasons and, though this

proved more challenging and uncomfortable, most of those that scored a 2. Mary came to accept that these reasons might have been important to her but ultimately not **that** important. They weren't individually or collectively going to convince her to stay or go. They had nudge power but not push power.

So she kicked them into touch.

What Joanne eliminated

It was the same with Joanne. She came up with all kinds of reasons for staying with her abusive partner that she scored 1 or 2. "He can be a laugh. He's good looking. Mum and Dad like him. He's better than her at things to do with the computer." But the fact that she scored them 1 or 2 and not 3 or even 3+ betrayed the fact that they were relatively light-weight factors that wouldn't ultimately sway her decision. Not that she saw it like this to begin with. It took a lot of talk, particularly with herself, to get to the point where she acknowledged this. Once she did, she accepted that there was no point in factoring them into her decision making any longer. Out they went.

What Emma and Greg eliminated

Emma and Greg didn't give many low scores for the arguments they exchanged about arrangements for Emma's mother. Each of them advanced a relatively small number of mainly (as they saw it) important points. Nonetheless, when we considered those that scored 2, there was general agreement about their lack of real impact on the decision they would need to come to. For example, Greg dropped his argument that his mother-in-law coming to stay would deprive their grown-up children of a room to stay. On reflection, he admitted that this seemed a bit selfish and disingenuous: he accepted that his children wouldn't complain and so the point didn't really have much potency.

For her part, Emma agreed that her argument that her mother might be mistreated if she were sent to the "wrong" care home was not a strong one since it was in their gift to make sure that she was sent to the "right" one. She dropped it as we whittled down the reasons being exchanged to get to the critical few and finally the critical one. However, after she and Greg agreed the path to take, she resurrected this reason, but in the form of a simple test question: *"Is this care home right for mum?"* At the post-decision stage it helped her implement the chosen course of action.

Letting go lets you get going—and learning

The elimination of minor reasons can be an uncomfortable process of letting go, but with each release there comes both greater enlightenment (a better appreciation of what really counts) and an associated lightness. The sense of feeling weighed down and conflicted begins to go away and there's an increasing laser-like focus upon the one or two things that do critically matter. Now you can really get moving towards the big decision.

You can learn a lot about what you really care about from the elimination process. Something might remain a value for you, but you realise that it's a lot less or a lot more important than you thought it was. By way of example, a former colleague and friend of mine discovered only after he had left his wife how much he cared about having a big TV set and how his "freedom" mattered a lot less to him than he imagined it would. Chances are he wouldn't have left had he known more clearly how much he cared for these and other things before he'd made the decision he came to regret.

By the way, if you can cope with (or benefit from) yet one more image of elimination, it is the exfoliation of an object: peeling back the outer layers of something like an onion to get to the heart or core of the issue. I know that some people like to work with this image.

Elimination works just as well for non-personal decisions

Let's illustrate elimination thinking in the professional as opposed to the personal field. One question asked frequently is: "Should we or shouldn't we offer this person a job?" This can be a big decision with many scary consequences if it's done badly. The basic elimination-based tool for initial selection is the person specification. This lists the requirements or conditions that have to be met. Applicants deemed not to meet the requirements are rejected—in theory, at least. It works much better if the criteria are prioritised because those failing to meet the critical few are eliminated quickly without the need to consider them further.

At one time, I advised governing bodies on the appointment of head teachers; and head teachers on the selection of teachers. On one occasion, the head teacher concerned was uncertain about whether or not to offer one of the candidates a job. This candidate had many things going for him but in an earlier assessment task he had shown very little ability to manage the behaviour of pupils. There was evidence that he had similar issues at his current school, and admitted as much to the interview panel. None of the training and support he had received had improved his behaviour management.

The head teacher sought to make a case for employing this very amiable man. "He's well qualified, he's enthusiastic, he's a music specialist, he's willing to run after-school clubs. He's got a lot going for him." I agreed, but questioned the head on whether any of these plus points were determining. I asked the head teacher two questions (i.e. applied two tests):

Is there any realistic prospect of this teacher acquiring the wherewithal to manage the behaviour of your many challenging students?

Would you really feel happy employing a teacher who you knew could not secure the basic conditions for creating a safe environment for teaching and learning?

The head said "no" to both, and that was that. All other considerations were immaterial: they would not have led the head teacher to change his mind.

The Killer Question

The head teacher reached the point where the decision was obvious. This is where the elimination process needs to get to. This is the quest of the questioning. So here's the most important sentence in this book:

> The best way to make a big, scary decision is to find the Killer Question.

If "Killer" sounds too dramatic and scary in itself, then you could call it the Crunch Question, the Hinge Question (because everything hinges on your response to it) or the Settlement Question, because its function is to settle the decision "once and for all". It's the question to which the answer is nearly always a straightforward "yes" or "no", and where the response is one of certainty. The Killer Question is the one test that will settle it for you. It could just as easily be called the Killer Test. Why "Killer"? Because it kills off further unnecessary deliberation. It lays it to rest. And your response to it? That's **The Killer Question Response.** It tells you what your decision needs to be.

Usually, there's little or no doubt about what the answer needs to be. The elimination process has filtered out all the arguments that are ultimately not going to determine the decision, not individually and rarely collectively. Add together all the minor considerations and they almost never matter more than the really big one captured by the Killer Question. I call them the "time wasters". Why? Because they have so little power to sway your decision that it's a waste of time lingering on them.

The best way to make a big decision is a quest: a quest to identify and formulate the Killer Question, the answer to which will determine the decision.

....

The Killer Question

Your response to this will tell you
what your decision needs to be.

....

Experience tells me that it's best for the quest to end in one question, but as in the school teacher example above, a pair of questions may be justified or even required. This pair nearly always has an "If... Then" structure. The first question prepares you for the second one. It sets out the crucial condition that needs to be met for you to be certain that the decision you are about to make is the right one. I call it "The Clincher" because it removes any doubt about what your response to the Killer Question has to be.

Responding with your mind and your body

Back to the Killer Question. Note that in the description above I use the word "response" rather than answer. And I use **Killer Question Response (KQR)** not Killer Answer. There's a good reason for that. "Answer" suggests a mind-only action whereas "response" includes mind and body. The KQR is Answer ++.

As I've indicated before, the sensations and feelings we get in our body are often strong and reliable guides to what our decisions should be. Our mind-body knows better than our mind alone. It sends us signals of comfort and discomfort and of certainty and uncertainty and we over-ride them at our peril. They are not always completely reliable, especially if we've spent a lot of our life over-riding the signals from our bodily intelligence. We can do this if, for example, they are inconvenient (they're telling us to slow down but we're telling ourselves we don't have the time) or we're repressing them because they're too painful to confront.

For a lot of us, our attention is so "out there" and we're operating solely from the neck up, that we are just not used to picking up on the more subtle signals our heart or gut or body more generally are sending us. Babies and young children are much more connected to their internal sensations. Reconnecting with the intelligence distributed around our whole mind-body is one of the critical keys to making decisions that are wiser and aligned to our overall best interests. If we are in touch with them, then they offer reliable signals to what our responses need to be.

Just one caveat. I'm not recommending that you rely upon gut feelings and similar types of mind-body signals to make decisions about external events. They really can't be relied upon to tell you who is going to win the 2.30 at Kempton race-course or which shares are going to rocket in value. More relevantly, they can't be relied upon to let you know that the house you're thinking of buying is worth the asking price or whether you'll easily find another job if you leave your current one. They can only have significant tell-tale value if they relate to something personal to you and which the mind-body system is party to.

Are there all-purpose Killer Questions?

This is an interesting question and I've worked with lots of individuals who have asked it in some form or another. They tend to suppose that there is an off-the-shelf Killer Question for their particular issue, the equivalent of a one-size-fits-all blood test. I've had people ask me this directly: "What's the Killer Question for deciding whether or not to change jobs?"

The short answer is that there isn't one. Everything depends upon the particular circumstances, concerns and wishes of the individual concerned. It can be a very different question for different individuals in seemingly similar situations. You have to devise and formulate a Killer Question, not pick one off the shelf, to be absolutely certain that it's precisely right for you.

Having said that, some people alight on the same Killer Question. I've identified over the years one or two questions that people are particularly drawn to and that seem to work particularly well for them. For people in "good" jobs, often well-regarded and well-paid jobs, the most frequently used Killer Question that I have experience of is a very simple one:

Does this job make my heart sing?

Before they or we have arrived at this question they've usually spent a lot of time weighing the pros and cons of their jobs. Considerations often include money (a good salary can often be a real sticking point even for the stressed and miserable), the demands upon them, the status of the job, its perceived worthwhile-ness and the security it offers. I've worked with people who have stayed in the same job for donkeys' years by virtue of being able to convince themselves, repeatedly, that the good points make leaving impossible.

But what I've also found is that when well-paid professionals ask themselves this stark but simple question—"Does this job make my heart sing?"—they know quickly what their honest response must be. It's a question that seems to confront individuals at a really profound level. I think it's because it goes directly to the heart rather than asking more vaguely about whether they like the job or whether it fits their talents. At the very specific physiological level, often there's a moment of almost shocked silence and stillness and a fixed stare. If the answer is a very clear "no" then it usually follows quickly and definitely. Several of the people I've coached have also, at that precise point, substituted "sink" for "swim". ("You must be joking! It makes my heart sink not swim.") They have a deep sense of its "wrongness" for them.

What I have also noticed is that if they answer "yes" or, more frequently, "sometimes", then they are likely to be motivated to take whatever action they can to improve their working lives to get the heart-singing experience more of the time. By contrast, if they respond with a fairly emphatic "no", as most people in unfulfilling job situations do, then no number of good points can compensate.

I don't think I've ever worked with someone who emphatically answered "no" but later changed their mind and returned to deliberating again. Some clients still had concerns about the consequences of leaving, or had to formulate a plan to shift job or career before feeling they could leave their current job, but their Killer Question gave them a clear direction for the future.

Now, I am not saying that "Does this job make my heart sing?" is the question you should address if you are contemplating a job move. It may or may not be. There is no one question that's exactly right for each person in this situation. Besides, some people feel they don't have, or they *really* don't have, any option but to stay in a job that makes their heart sink. All I am saying is that this is the question that's done the business for a number of the people I've worked with. (A lot of those people, I have to say, were fortunate enough to be in circumstances that enabled them to go with their heart rather than put up with a job they didn't like just so they could put food on the table or fit in with their kids' schooling. Not everyone's so lucky, of course, so might have to use "Does this job make my heart sing?" as a motivational spur to finding the right Killer Question for them.)

As I've indicated, finding the right-for-you Killer Question is a quest. Some people end it quickly because they identify the Killer Question quickly and effortlessly. It can come in a moment of inspiration or emerge because at some level the person already knows what that question is but has allowed it to stay half buried. It can be scary to confront a question that's stark and potentially life-altering. It can take your breath away.

For most people, the quest is a journey that begins when deliberating on the pros and cons leads nowhere and attention shifts to searching for the genuine Killer Question. This usually involves experimenting with questions that don't prove killer enough. They may miss the target completely (i.e. focus on something that really isn't significant enough to be decisive) but often they are versions of the same theme or even the same question.

For example, I've witnessed several individuals try out "false" (i.e. unsuccessful) Killer Questions for sorting the job-changing dilemma. One of these questions is:

Is this a job worth devoting my time to?

On the face of it, this question seems similar to the heart sing question in terms of what it gets the individual to confront. But actually it works very differently. The heart sing question takes the individual inside and tends to elicit a response that locates deep feelings. They sense at a heart, soul or even cellular level whether they are engaged in work that is both thrilling and personally meaningful.

When someone asks themselves "Is this a job worth devoting my time to?" they start to consider the "worthy-ness" or "worthwhile-ness" of the job. They say things such as, "This is an important job. It matters to a lot of people." They may talk about having the skills and talent for the job. But none of this may be critically determining. They can have the talent for a job but not value it or get excited using it. They might be great at playing the violin or at teaching but not want to stay in their job as a violinist or as a teacher.

They can know that a job is important and worthwhile, but no longer feel that it is for them. In my experience, *"Is this job worthy of devoting my time to?"* is rarely an effective Killer Question. It is, though, a possible precursor to the "Does this job make my heart sing?" question. Finding *the* "Right" question after toying with one that isn't can make the discovery even more impactful.

Before we leave this section and consider how finding the right Killer Question is often a process of experimentation and discovery, I want to suggest one question worth getting into the habit of asking time and time again. It's not a Killer Question, as such, but it has full-spectrum value and can be used in just about any situation to ease the mind into identifying the Killer Question.

For me, the very best question to make your default, so that you ask it automatically in any relevant situation, is this:

What are my options here?

or

What alternatives do I have?

When we have a tough decision to make under tough conditions, it's very easy to freeze and feel trapped. Our mind closes to all but one of two possibilities. This doesn't make us resourceful. If we ask "What are my options here?" our brain has to generate other possibilities, one or some of which might be much better than the first thing we thought of. It also makes us feel calmer and more in control because we're not forced down one path only. Having options liberates.

There are times when a decision has to be made in an instant. On these occasions, decisiveness trumps decision quality: it's better to do something than nothing or faffing. But such times are rare, and often the best quality decisions come from options thinking. And, what's particularly relevant here, as I've suggested, is that options thinking can be a great precursor to deciding The Killer Question.

Experiment—and get the benefits

Sometimes, arriving at exactly the right question requires patience and a willingness to experiment. That's the nature of the quest and utterly worth the effort. The great virtue is that it's a highly focussed quest and trying out alternative versions and formulations can make the journey even more focussed. It can illuminate priorities within the priorities, because with hard-to-make decisions there are often competing priorities. You thought X was the number one priority but you've come to the conclusion that it's actually Y. Or, if it's a group decision, there may be differing views about the priorities.

Let's look at two examples.

The fate of Mum's doll's house

The first involves a family; in particular, a brother and sister, both in their 50s. The brother has debts following a recent divorce. His sister is just slightly better off, but her job as a care worker means that money is always tight for her. Their mother has recently died and has passed onto them the only really valuable thing she owned: a Victorian doll's house with all the original figures and items of furniture inside. They believe it is highly valuable; it may not be, but that's hardly relevant. The question the siblings have to wrestle with is whether to keep or sell the doll's house. On the one hand, they knew their mother cherished it and they themselves played with it as children and so it has a lot of sentimental value. On the other, they could both do with the money it could make at auction.

They began their decision-making with the usual kind of debating. With themselves or each other? It really didn't matter, but as it happened, both.

It has so many memories.

Yes, but we can't live on memories.

As usual, juggling pros and cons didn't get them very far. When they started to think in terms of the question that would settle it for them, they experimented with several, including slight but possibly significant versions of the same one. Here are the main contenders generated in largely this order:

Can we cope with our feelings of loss and guilt if we sell it?

Will the feelings of loss and guilt soon outweigh any of the good the money does us?

What will bring us the greatest benefits in the long-term?

What will give us most peace of mind in the future?

What would mum tell us to do?

What would mum want us to do?

The deliberation focussed so much on what the siblings would lose if they sold the doll's house that it was fairly certain which decision they were inclined towards. But finding the question that would enable them to exit and put the deliberation behind them, was still a challenge.

With each of the first four questions, they thought they had found the clincher. But since they kept on talking, evidently not. Then they came up with the penultimate question, the one that's fifth in the list above: "What would mum tell us to do?" They were certain that the answer to this was to sell the doll's house and benefit from the money it might bring them.

She was, after all, a very caring mum and aware that she was leaving nothing else of real monetary value.

But that assumed answer did not sit well with them; their insides felt uncomfortable. Finally, they changed just one word, but a critical one: they substituted "want" for "tell". And they knew immediately that their mum would really want them to keep the doll's house in the family and for it to be passed down the generations. They knew she'd say one thing but mean another. That settled it for them. It was in line with the thrust of their thinking (the short-term monetary benefits would soon be forgotten but the emotional costs wouldn't) and was just the right Killer Question for them.

Luke's future

The second example is again family-based. Heather and Trevor are the parents of 11 year-old Luke. They live in a part of the country where the selective education system still exists; some time back they wanted Luke to take the 11+ exam to try to get into the local grammar school. Luke wasn't particularly keen, but went along with his parents' wishes. When the results of the 11+ came out, Heather and Trevor were told that their son had not been successful: he was a few marks away from achieving the score necessary. The issue they had to decide is: Shall we appeal against the decision? Parents can do this and some are "successful". When they discussed this with the head teacher of Luke's primary school they were told (not for the first time) that Luke might struggle at grammar school, especially because of his challenges with both maths and English. They were also reminded of some local, well-rated wide-ability schools.

Heather and Trevor tried to decide what to do by finding the right question to settle the matter. The question they'd fixated on all along is "How can we get Luke into grammar school?" That goal continued to drive them, so the first question they came up with was:

Should we make an appeal and pay for a private tutor for Luke if the appeal is successful?

When Luke told his parents that he wasn't keen on this and

that a lot of his friends were going to one of the wide-ability schools, they started to think again. Heather had not been able to forget a word that the head teacher had used: "flourish", and she suggested to her husband that they'd be better off asking the following question:

At which school is Luke most likely to flourish?

Luke had visited other local schools and knew which one he thought would suit him best. The final question they used to decide included (rightly) Luke's views:

At which school do we all feel that Luke is most likely to flourish?

That became their Killer Question. It might seem odd that this was not the obvious question to ask from the outset, but one thing I've learned is that people often take a long time to formulate what most onlookers would regard as "no brainers". The quest to find the right Killer Questions can involve big shifts in perspective and ways in which the situation is defined. To those detached from the situation, it can often seem like the discovery of common sense, or finding the question that should have been staring the deliberators in the face all along.

Luke's father, in particular, was so wedded to the idea that his son should go to a grammar school that shifting his perspective from the school to Luke's lived experience of it did not come easily. When he made that shift securely he spent some time beating himself up about not putting his son's capacity to thrive centre-stage from the outset.

That's another possible result of finding a Killer Question that I've observed a lot: those concerned think it should have been obvious to them at the outset, and feel some guilt or embarrassment that it wasn't. That's even more the case when the Killer Question turns out to be a very simple one such as: Will leaving make **anyone** happy? I tell them that sometimes we need to be like an inter-continental ballistic missile—not going straight to the target but zig-zagging to it. That can have unexpected benefits, including discovering things we might not have done had we got to it straight away. The process of making a really tough decision is so often a learning journey. After we've made it, we can sometimes feel blessed that it took us all around the houses, some familiar and some not so.

It All Depends...

Finding the right Killer Question is a quest that ends infuriating ambivalence and uncertainty. When you've found it, you've found your personal Holy Grail, so it pays to be patient and persistent. That might mean, as we've said, trying out a number of different questions, all but one of which you will eliminate. Having a clear sense of what we might call the heart of the matter—the truly core concern—can make the process more efficient.

Take the "Shall we stay in this house or move?" type decision familiar to thousands of people at any one time. It's another one of those situations that can drag on torturously and unresolved for ages. Again, there is no one right Killer Question. The right one depends upon the particular issues and circumstances, but above all the core one. In other words, it all depends.

Here are a few of the Killer Questions I've helped to draw out of people I've been involved with. Each of them reflects the core issue.

Q. Will the house we are in now be right for us in the long term?

The middle-aged couple who asked themselves this had children at university who they thought might return to live at home and elderly parents that would probably need to be accommodated in the future. They knew that this was precisely the right question to address and knew, sadly (because they loved their current house) that the answer had to be "no".

Q. Are we determined enough to move to cough up as much as £10,000 to make our house more saleable even if it's not more valuable?

This couple had a house that they had failed to maintain and was in a poor state of repair. Estate agents told them, correctly they assumed, that it would be difficult to sell if they didn't get it up to scratch, but that the work would not substantially increase the market value of their property. The couple's thinking had looped for a long time because they couldn't get their focus away from the question of whether they were happy to spend a lot of money "for the benefit of strangers" as they put it. Indeed, the first version of this question was: "Are we prepared to spend £10,000 to make our house more saleable but scarcely more valuable?" Only when they focussed upon what they really wanted for themselves (moving at all costs) did they get to the question that sorted their decision. Their answer was "yes".

Q. Is the change to our outlook bad enough for us to look at other houses we might want to move to?

This is another Killer Question with earlier iterations. The elderly sisters who addressed this question had lived in their much-loved property for over 40 years, and had always enjoyed uninterrupted views across open, edge-of-town countryside. Now a housing estate was being built on the land opposite and they were devastated to think their outlook would be blighted.

At first, they simply asked: "Should we move?" but found themselves going around in circles when they discussed it. We shifted the question to: "Is the change in outlook bad enough to make us move?" To begin with, that seemed like the Killer Question, but it was too stark, almost intimidating, for the elderly sisters, especially the use of "make us". They were not sure if they had the energy to make a move or if there was any house they could like as much as their current one. The question immobilised them more than it galvanised them, so we tweaked it to commit them (if they chose to answer "yes") to exploring the possibility of moving without committing them to do so. This question energised them and they were quick to say "yes".

This example also illustrates something else: finding the Killer Question can move you to the next stage, but it might not be the final stage. Getting there might require a different question. But often we only have enough energy or vision or wherewithal to move forward one stage. That's usually fine. If you're in that position, then as long as you are not simply kicking the can down the road so you don't have to deal with the crunch situation, then usually that's facilitative rather than avoidant. Making several Killer Questions can even build the Killer Question muscle. It can be a good thing.

You might be wondering what Killer Questions sealed the deal for the individuals I spoke about earlier. Well, here they are:

Mary's Killer Question

Am I prepared to spend the rest of my life with a man I don't love and doesn't show he loves or cares for me?

Joanne's Killer Question

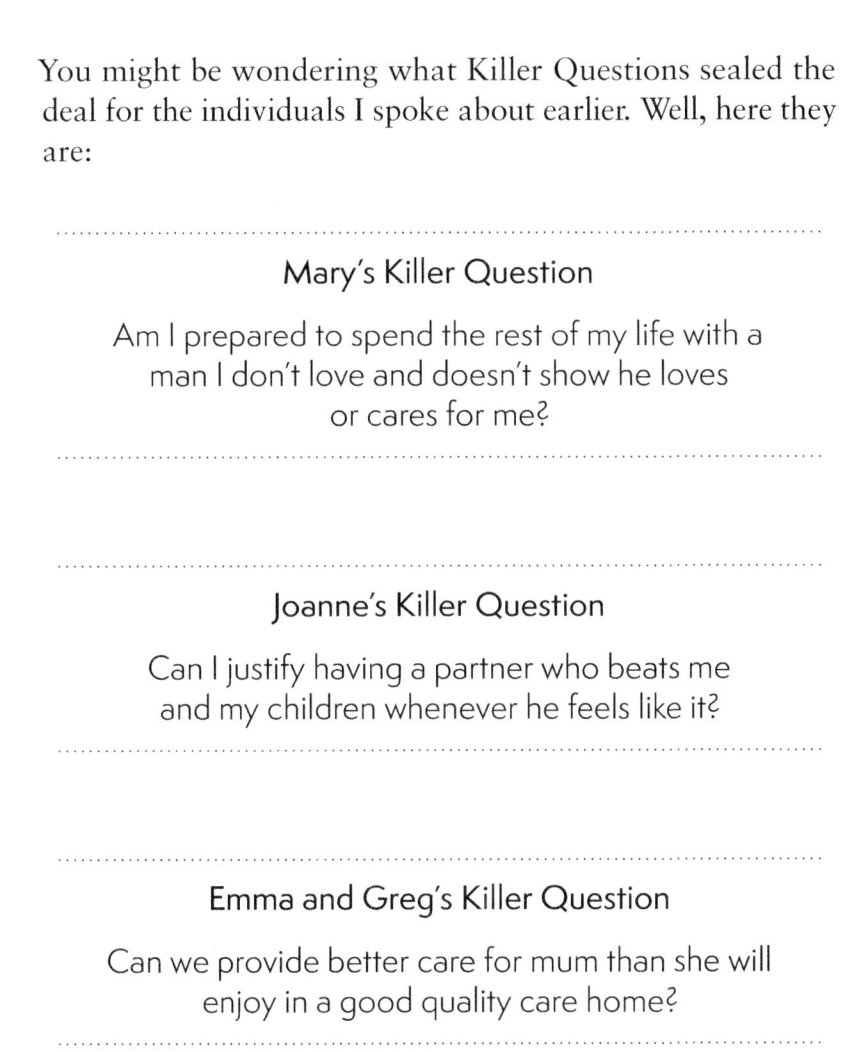

Can I justify having a partner who beats me and my children whenever he feels like it?

Emma and Greg's Killer Question

Can we provide better care for mum than she will enjoy in a good quality care home?

You may be surprised by how simple and seemingly obvious these Killer Questions are. You might be wondering why it was so challenging for the people concerned to formulate them. But the truth is, it was. Particularly all the time they were locked into a pros and cons approach AND felt they ought to consider every possible pro and con, no matter how unlikely many were to influence their decision. Even the most obvious route can be obscured when you can't see the wood for the trees.

If you keep going back to individual "trees", to all the minor considerations that are really incidentals because they won't swing your decision one way or the other, then it's easy to lose your central focus. You might even have come up with something like the Killer Question early in your deliberations but it seemed too simple, or you couldn't stop yourself over thinking. So you dismissed it. That was pretty much Mary's situation. It didn't really take her the best part of three decades to decide that staying with someone you don't love and who doesn't love you might not be a wise thing to do. But it did take her that long to keep her focus on that and not be swayed by minor factors that amounted to very little in the bigger scheme of things.

What you don't see when you look at a Killer Question is all the fat that's been stripped away to leave a question that is strikingly lean. Most Killer Questions are like those above: short, straightforward, stark and single-focussed. You don't need many words to tell the truth or to elicit it. And ultimately that's what the Killer Question is designed to do: capture the truth of a situation by identifying the critical factor at its heart.

The Clincher Convincer

Let's supposing you have a good idea of what the Killer Question is. And maybe you also know what your response to it is or should be, but you are still not acting upon it. What you need is an experience that clinches it for you, one that seals the deal, as it were. It's a "tipping point" experience. The verbal equivalent is: *"Right! That's it!"* Or:

"Enough is enough!"

The clincher experience can be unwelcome on one level if it's unpleasant, humiliating or worse, but since it "tips you over the edge" it's something you come to be grateful for. But it can also be a very minor episode that becomes the "last straw." It's not something you've orchestrated or planned for; it just happens. Here's an example:

Years ago I was talking with a middle-aged gay man called Nathan. He told me that he'd recently ended a two year relationship with a much younger man who had been "taking him for a ride". Nathan knew the reality of the situation but had been "besotted" with the younger man. "What possessed me to put up with a selfish and exploitative boyfriend?" he asked, so he'd come close to formulating his own Killer Question. I asked him what finally clinched it for him. He told me that "it was something quite small." Nathan had asked his boyfriend to record a TV programme that he really wanted to watch (at a time when a live recording was the only option). When Nathan got home his boyfriend said he'd forgotten to record it and showed no regret or concern. Nathan said he calmly told his boyfriend to pack his belongings, get out and never come back.

Spur-of-the-moment decision-making can be impulsive and something we come to regret. But often it's just what we need to push us into doing what we've already decided is in our best interests. This was clearly the case with Nathan.

How do you know if it's the right response or an impetuous one you'll come to rue? You know that it's the right one if it's in line with what you have already decided is the right thing to do. We can shock even ourselves when we act decisively in the moment, and the timing may not be ideal, but the sensation is overwhelmingly one of relief rather than regret. At least, that's what I've observed time and again.

Step 5: Testing You've Got It Right

How do you know if you've identified The Killer Question?

I think we've come close to answering this, but let's reiterate the main point: it's through your whole mind-body intelligence.

- You get a strong internal conviction

- This usually includes a feeling of certainty in the gut and/or elsewhere

- You benefit from the contrast effect

This last point means that you know that the response you get from Killer Question is significant because it's noticeably different from that you've got from other questions. It's often subtly but strongly different. It's the contrast that makes it impactful. You probably feel that now all parts of you are speaking with a single voice and no longer debating with themselves. Your precise physiology may also be different. For example, you may be gazing calmly ahead rather than moving your eyes from side to side. You may experience a bodily stillness you didn't when you formulated other questions, or something close to its opposite: raised level of excitement—the kind you get when you have an epiphany or you make a sudden breakthrough. Clarity and certainty come from sensing that your response differs significantly from your responses to other questions.

Of course, it's not just about sensations and physiology. You also know at a mental level that the Killer Question is the one you need to address above all others. It provides the supreme test for the action you should take.

What adds to your conviction? It could be that it's pointing you in the direction you knew all along you'd need to take but didn't want to acknowledge or accept. Nathan knew all along that his boyfriend was in the relationship for his own selfish ends. Nathan's informal version of a Killer Question compelled him to confront this reality. Joanne sensed all along that she couldn't pull a veil over her boyfriend's violent outbursts, but it took the starkness of the Killer Question to finally accept it.

The Killer Question as Discovery

Or it could be that the Killer Question centres on something that has moved ineluctably from the periphery to centre stage as you've engaged with it. A surprise epiphany can be as convincing as recognition. You didn't see it as determining and now you do. You were virtually blind to it; now it seems blindingly obvious. Someone says how much they love their job and suddenly, in that moment you realise how much you don't love yours.

Astonishing as it may seem, I've known several high-achieving individuals, torn between staying or leaving well-paid jobs, who have not recognised how little they now resonated with or valued their job. They've given lots of reasons for leaving (more family time, a tiresome commute, pressures from above) but failed to realise how little their actual work had come to mean to them. Only when forced to confront the matter has it dawned on them, and sometimes become their Killer Question.

You've addressed your Killer Question and made your decision: What Now?

Finding the Killer Question, and knowing what your decision surely has to be, marks the beginning of the end. The end comes when you've actually acted on the decision you've made. So how can you best prepare for turning decision into action? In other words, how can you make it all work?

First, **manage your expectations.** The Killer Question isn't a piece of magic. It won't necessarily solve all your issues or waft you to a bed of roses. **Don't expect any new sense of certainty to end all the discomfort.** There could still be painful times ahead, so the best thing you can do for yourself is to get comfortable being uncomfortable. Accept the practical and emotional difficulties your decision might bring in its wake. If you've decided to leave an unhappy marriage (as Mary did) or to place your ailing parent in a care home (as did Emma and Greg) then you're going to have to put up with a period of making arrangements that might prove tricky and meet with opposition. And you could well have a nagging sense of guilt even if you know you've made the best all-round decision.

Holding your nerve could be a challenge. If you lose it, you could coward out and return to a state of miserable ambivalence.

Now, here is a REALLY important point: experience tells me

that the **number one reason people make poor decisions—ones they almost certainly know at the time are wrong—is that they are unwilling to put up with the short-term discomfort that goes with making the right decision.** They swap long-term wellbeing for short-term pain-avoidance.

> Following through with your response to The Killer Question may take courage and a willingness to put up with short-term discomfort.

Supposing you decide to leave a secure, well-paid job and your family think you are mad for doing so. Chances are, you'll feel stressed as well as relieved, and you'll get some grief before landing a job that is right for you. If you commit to leaving a relationship that is ultimately wrong for you, or commit to making a challenging relationship work in the long-term, then you can't expect everything to be hunky-dory immediately. You're going to have some tough times first.

So, critical to making and keeping the right decisions is a willingness to put up with unpleasant stuff in the short-term. As far as big, scary decisions are concerned, it's unlikely you'll gain without pain. It might be emotional pain—other people trying to make you feel guilty, for example, or witnessing the suffering your decision is bringing others. It might be actual threats to your wellbeing (from, say, abusive partners or antagonistic colleagues). It might be financial loss or insecurity.

Keeping your focus upon the potential prize ahead (attaining the dream, peace of mind, a better relationship or whatever else your decision is moving you towards) is key to surviving the interim challenges. Doing this is in line with the stress management principle that says: if the source of your stress is in the present, then put your mind on the future you're hoping for. (It's the opposite when the source of the stress is in the future.) This will help to keep you buoyant.

When Mary made her exceptionally late-coming decision to leave her husband, she felt relief and a peace she hadn't known for 30 years, but the aftermath was frightening for her. She had to make all kinds of practical arrangements, worry about finances and deal with the fall-out from some members of her family. But she also knew that in the long-term her decision would prove the right one. Joanne and Emma and Greg felt something very similar.

Have a plan, or incorporate a commitment to planning within your Killer Question.

One reason people are scared of making big decisions is that the aftermath looks too much like a **cliff edge**. One minute you're in a relationship or a job or a house or whatever, and then the Killer Question commits you to a sudden and possibly traumatic change. That's scary.

But it seems less scary if you have a plan that makes the shift look more like a gentle incline than a cliff edge. If you build this into the Killer Question, then it can certainly soften the blow of making the right but still very challenging commitment. You're more likely to say "yes" to leaving a job you hate or a marriage that's failing if you have a fairly clear idea of how you plan to do so. (Sadly, you are also more likely to go through with a decision to commit suicide if you have at least a two-step plan of action.)

To reach what I call our personal **confidence threshold,** some of us will need a detailed plan with time-scales and specific actions and details built into it. Some of us will just need to know that we have some idea of how things will proceed and, hopefully, work out well.

You're going to move forward with greater vim and vigour if you know what you need in order to feel confident. Do yourself a big favour and work out what you require to reach your threshold: at one extreme, it could be a full-length video in your head of everything you'll need to do to execute the decision; at the other, just a general feeling that you will confidently tackle whatever comes up.

What I have found is that a Killer Question with a generous time-scale for delivery built in can make it easier to commit to fully. The implementation time offers breathing space. The cliff edge may still be there (the moment you actually leave the marital home, for example) but it's a fair way off and so less alarming. There's time to make the necessary arrangements and adjustments that will make it as smooth and manageable as possible. Here's an example.

John's departure

John was a very "successful" insurance broker, but felt increasingly stressed by and trapped in his job. He had a long commute each day and saw far too little of his wife and children. He also knew that his job was impacting on his health and wellbeing. I'll never forget his comment that each day he had to put more and more into a job that he felt less and less like doing. The trouble was that his very well-paid job was funding a life-style that was costly but no longer serving his best interests or those of his wife and children.

When I met John he told me that after more than 15 years in finance he wanted to do something "more meaningful" (train as a teacher) but that would mean drastic changes that (in his words) he "couldn't justify". Fortunately, Lena, John's wife, was more concerned about her husband's well-being and their family life than she was about maintaining a lavish life-style. So together and with me they honed a Killer Question that helped them to make the decision they knew was right.

"Honed" is the right word. Their early attempts did not immediately fill them with joyful commitment even though they captured the general sense of the final question. Semantics mattered, as they so often do when formulating the Killer Question. They began by talking about "giving up" and "making sacrifices" to the way they lived, but that didn't work. Everything smelled of loss. They substituted "making adjustments" and that felt much better. But most critical was the addition of an extended timescale for preparation and implementation.

The penultimate version was this:

Are we as a family o.k. about making adjustments to the way we live so that Dad can quit his job and retrain as a teacher?

The family said "yes" but were obviously tentative. When we spoke about it what emerged was the concern that this would involve a sudden "overnight" change. So the final question that became the Killer Question included a section that allayed that concern and made them all feel able to commit to it confidently. The Killer Question was this:

Are we as family o.k. about making gradual adjustments to the way we live so that Dad can make plans to retrain as a teacher in September next year?

When people are understandably nervous about making big life changes, even if they have a profound sense that they need to make them, then it can help considerably if the Killer Question is more "soft" than "hard". Putting in breathing space is one way to do this. If the implementation is either gradual or some way off, then they don't have to feel rushed and pressured.

Cliff-edge avoidance is not always easy or possible. Individuals who've thought long and hard about whether to speak out about something that's really concerned them can go from under-the-radar anonymity one day to having the spotlight of public scrutiny on them the next. That can be terrifying and traumatic. What can help is some aftermath planning: anticipating reactions, preparing their responses to them and doing some scenario planning before they leap so they have at least a degree of confidence about managing whatever occurs.

Even if possible, time delay is not always the right thing to do. Rapid follow-through is absolutely necessary in some situations (as it was for Joanne suffering domestic abuse). Also, if a "breathing space" offers an escape hatch or a get-out clause (ie an excuse not to act upon the decision) then it can be totally counter-productive. But if it helps it seal the deal, then it can reduce the fearful resistance that sometimes prevents bold but right decisions being made. Reasonable or even generous time horizons for acting on the decision can make all the difference to the level of commitment it enjoys.

Keep looking ahead

The other golden key to implementing the decision you've made is to **not look back**. Once you've made up your mind, stop any further deliberation. The time for that has passed. And, if you feel that the right decision has been made, then so also has the need. As I said earlier, minds are made to close as well as to open. At this stage you benefit from being blinkered.

It helps to make two decisions when you respond to your Killer Question. The first is a "yes" or a "no". The other is a decision to commit to the first decision and not to look back or over at the path not chosen. This is the same commitment I suggested for post-FOTS decisions.

Resisting the impulse to look back takes discipline, and one of the best things you can do for your effectiveness as a decision-maker is to cultivate more of it. You do this by practicing not thinking about the path or paths not taken whenever you have a fork-in-the-road choice to make. You can do this with everyday choices, such as the choice of one birthday gift for someone rather than another, or one curtain fabric rather than another. If through daily practice you can wean yourself off the temptation to question your decisions after you've made them, then you are making life a lot easier for yourself.

What do you do when a little voice in your head whispers: "Yes, but what if?" Or you get a mental picture of the path not taken? What you do is re-focus. You bring your focus back to the path you have taken and you picture that. You might want to reinforce that with talking to yourself—out loud or in your head—about that path. And if necessary you do that more than once, in fact, as many times as necessary.

Looking back and speculating on what might have been is usually pointless. Worse still, "what ifs?" and regret make you anxious, weaken your resolve and suck your energy. Don't indulge in them unless there is a realistic possibility of finding a way to take the path not originally chosen (i.e. reversing your decision) and you seriously believe it's the better option.

After you've made a big, scary decision the best thing to do is focus on the future.

So: **Don't Look Back**

High Level Killer Questions

There's no obvious place to put this short section, so I'm dealing with it here.

I said earlier that Killer Questions aren't magic. Coming up with one isn't like waving a magic wand and miracles happen. This is generally true. But some Killer Questions can work a kind of magic. These are the ones that address not just the immediate issue but also, potentially, a whole bunch of other entangled issues. This is the case if the Killer Question is high level, if it sits at the top of a pile of other issues at different levels.

The best image for this is a hierarchy or pyramid made up of several levels with level one being the bottom level. In theory, at least, solving issues at level 2 should also solve those they subsume at level one, in much the same way as a bigger Russian doll contains and includes a smaller one. Solving issues at level 3 should resolve the issues at both levels below it because they subsume those issues. And so on.

If the Killer Question is at the apex of the pyramid, then it should be able to resolve or dissolve all the issues below it—to some extent, at least.

(If it works better for you, then you could go for a depth image by inverting the pyramid and talking about the "root" of a problem. The branched network above it are the equivalent of the levels. I'll concentrate on the top-down levels model.)

It might seem complicated but in essence it isn't. You've probably had your own experiences of this. For example, you have a whole range of problems—physical, mental, financial, relational etc—that are all linked to your job and more or less disappear when you change it. Or all your family problems are sorted when one member of it either leaves or becomes a very different kind of person.

There's a technique called the "Five Whys" that can sometimes get you to the highest level question/solution. It presupposes a five level hierarchy and the answer to each question takes you one level up. Here's an example: (It is only an example and in no way meant to be anti-school.)

> Q. *Why have all the bins in this school playground been bashed in?*
>
> A. *Because the pupils are bored and taking their frustration out on the bins.*
>
> Q. *Why are they bored?*
>
> A. *Because the curriculum doesn't engage them.*

Q. Why doesn't the curriculum engage them?

A. Because the staff don't make it engaging.

Q. Why don't the staff make it engaging?

A. Because they aren't motivated enough to put in the effort.

Q. Why not?

A. Because the leadership are autocratic and bullying, so do nothing to make the staff feel valued and empowered.

So the high level solution is, obviously, to change the leadership or change the way it operates. This should fix all the problems to which it gives rise. (Actually, this might not be the highest level solution. We could go on and ask why the leadership are autocratic and bullying and answer that they are themselves being pressured/bullied by, say, their Academy Trust bosses and/or the Government. But sometimes you have to settle for the highest level over which you have some control.)

Let's consider some Killer Question equivalents. Sometimes, the best Killer Question comes about by tweaking lower level iterations. This nudges it up a level. We've already had examples of this. Recall Luke and his parents who wanted to get him into grammar school. The questions they asked at an early stage didn't hit the mark. The penultimate question they considered was: "At which school is Luke most likely to flourish?" The final question they asked was: "At which school do we all feel that Luke is most likely to flourish?"

This question included the views of Luke himself, so was the higher level question—and all the better for it. Had the parents bypassed Luke they might have had a "Luke issue" that remained unresolved, quite possible if he felt resentful or devalued because his views had not been sought.

Something very interesting about the high level killer question is that the response doesn't need to be deep and profound. It can be simple or profoundly simple. It can be at a high level of abstraction but the answer can be concrete. Here's a very memorable illustration.

At a high-rise office block in New York, all VPs and other top executives had their plush offices and suites on the top floor. But they were very disgruntled by the length of the time it took for the elevator to get to them. They'd press for the elevator to come and it might arrive 30 or more seconds later. That made them very frustrated. They thought they were too important to be made to wait that long. The solution they proposed was the construction of another elevator, probably on the outside of the tower block. The cost of this would have been astronomical. Some savvy soul invited a psychologist friend to look at the situation and see if she could come up with any alternative recommendation. She did.

What enabled her to do so? Rather than accept the question the company executives had been assuming: "How can we cut down waiting time for the elevator?", she posed her own Killer Question: "How can we make the executives o.k. about waiting for the elevator?"

What she proposed was the installation of some large, attractive mirrors next to the elevator doors where the big cheeses waited. Her reasoning for this decision? She observed how vain or narcissistic most of them seemed to be and concluded that they would be happy preening themselves in front of the mirrors and so would barely notice the waiting times they were complaining about. Her recommendation was accepted and her assumptions proved more or less spot on. There were one or two unhappy souls, but most only ever complained mildly and sporadically.

I love this story and the ridiculously practical, low-cost solution of preening mirrors. Some personal and professional problems can also be sorted by straightforward practical solutions. A question always worth asking is, "Is there a relatively simple, practical solution to this dilemma?" even if the prospect of finding one seems remote. Killer Questions like this are the equivalent of sprats to catch mackerels or a lot of bang for your bucks—potentially great returns on investment.

In the next chapter I'm going to suggest coin tossing as possible decision-making strategy. You can't get much more simple and practical than this. There are others. One that has sometimes emerged is a "taster experience." I once encountered a graduate who had been offered a job in the UAE. She had several concerns which made it difficult for her to make up her mind, but the biggest was the heat of the climate in the UAE. She came from a working-class Welsh family, had spent childhood holidays at Tenby and had never been abroad, let alone to anywhere really hot. It wasn't the final Killer Question, but she kept asking, "How can I know if I will cope with the heat?" The simple solution suggested by a friend was that she should try out the sauna in a local health club. If she could cope with that, then Dubai shouldn't be a problem. I don't know the outcome, but I know she was up for that proxy experience, and it could well have helped her decide about the job offer.

Long before coronavirus-induced lockdowns, I often worked with individuals stressed by daily commutes and work/life balance issues. The big decision for many was whether to leave well-paid jobs they actually rather liked. Initially, their thinking was mainly about what other jobs they could do and whether they could survive on lower salaries or where they could re-locate to. The idea of a different mode of working didn't always occur to them. After discussion, a number opted for a Killer Question on the lines of: "How can I keep the job but change how I do it so that I am no longer so stressed?"

It seems such an obvious question to pose, especially for all those who've been through a pandemic-induced lockdown and the experience of working from home (WFH). But it was not so obvious to those who equated going to work with commuting, and were too stressed even to imagine other possibilities. The idea of negotiating the possibility of doing at least some of their work from home did not immediately occur to everyone, especially those employed by companies where WFH was not common practice.

Asking and being allowed to WFH for at least two or three days a week was a straightforward practical solution with several benefits.

Chapter 6

The Killer Question for helpers

I've written this book from the perspective of someone with a professional as well as a personal interest in helping other people make tough decisions. I've helped friends, family members and plenty of other individuals to make decisions, and done so, of course, informally. But the basis of this book is the experience I've had as a decision-making coach and trainer. I've made a bit of a speciality of decision-making, but almost anyone in one of the "helping professions" will be involved in providing some level of decision-making service to their clients or (and I hate the term) their service users. I'm thinking of counsellors, psychotherapists, life coaches, executive coaches, mentors, consultants of various kinds and almost anyone with an advisory, supervisory or managerial job of some description. Assisting individuals to make decisions may not even be in their job descriptions, but it will very likely figure in what they actually do.

Much of what I say in this book about decision-making for

couples, families and individuals in their personal capacities applies equally to those with a more formal or professional relationship to others. But some aspects of decision-making are peculiar to particular groups of professional helpers, so I am going to say a little about two of these: agony columnists and coaches.

Agony Aunts and Uncles

When we have an issue we're really struggling with, we might seek the advice of an Agony Aunt or Uncle. Newspapers and some magazines still employ them and they are very popular with both advice-seekers and general readers. One reason people turn to Agony columnists is that they think they kind of know them, because some are celebrities in their own right, or because they've been reading their columns for a long time and so feel they are familiar figures. At the same time, the letter/email writers know that the columnists do not know them personally, so confidentiality and being identified are not things they have to worry about. Most obviously, people at their wits' end, unable or unwilling to make a decision, often have no one else to turn to or, at least, no one they fully trust.

I've not had many dealings with people who have written to Agony Aunts or Uncles in national publications and had their letters printed, but I do know some who have had responses from local newspaper columnists and various unofficial Agony Aunts. Some of these individuals found the replies helpful without ending their quandaries. The responses gave them things to consider that they hadn't thought about before, but didn't lead them conclusively to a firm decision. Some got responses that they didn't find helpful. The reasons here are interesting. Some simply didn't like the advice they were being offered. They thought it demanded too much of them or was simply unpalatable. But some were left disappointed and frustrated because they thought it missed the mark, that it didn't somehow capture the heart of the problem.

Here's my thinking: giving someone in a dilemma a simple "do this" or "think about this" response probably wouldn't be the right thing to do, though I have certainly coached people who wanted just this—someone else to tell them exactly what to do. Bewilderment often leads to willing infantilism.

Usually, the kinds of issues people present to agony columnists have some complexity about them and so it is totally legitimate for the columnists to unpack their thinking and encourage the individual to ponder a number of things in order to make, if it's relevant, a definite decision. But what if every Agony Aunt and Uncle were required to identify what they thought the Killer Question might be—or alternative Killer Questions, though this might give them too much leeway and let them off the hook of piercing the heart of the matter?

I'm not suggesting an either/or here. The columnist wouldn't need to choose between a Killer Question or a discursive response. They could still set out their thinking and make their suggestions, but they would also be required to formulate a Killer Question that seemed to them the principal question their letter-writer should be addressing. They might even make it explicit, and say: "This is the question I/we think you most need to address, and your answer to it should strongly suggest the decision/action you need to take."

If Agony Aunts and Uncles accepted the challenge I am suggesting, then it would be one way to assess their emotional intelligence and their ability to identify the crux of the matter. If they can formulate a Killer Question that enables the person with the problem to make the decision that would resolve it or, at least, move forward with confidence, then that would surely be some mark of their quality. If they can't do this, then it perhaps suggests that they haven't really understood the issue and their analysis is faulty or fuzzy. Or perhaps it suggests that the columnist is reluctant to challenge the correspondent or their definition of the situation, for that's what the Killer Question quite often is. It's a challenge that the person concerned would rather not accept even if they know or sense that it's one they need to face.

None of the above is meant as an attack on agony columnists. The situations some people need help with are often very messy and sometimes situations they seem to be stuck with. I suspect that in response to some readers' plights, the agony columnists are more concerned with hitting the right empathic note than prescribing action.

I'm sure also that many of them do try to formulate the questions that will be most helpful to those they are trying to help. Their advice might have perceived value even if they don't do this. As I've hinted, some people who write to agony columnists don't want "the truth" or to be confronted with insights and suggestions that discomfort them. And I'm sure that a lot of columnists go very easy on their correspondents because they sense their pain and fragility and don't want to leave them with even more challenges to cope with. Highly empathic agony columnists almost certainly aim to calibrate their responses so that they are hard-hitting with those they deem can take it and softer with those they sense can't. But my own view is that they should in general aim to get to the heart of the individual's situation and show this in a question that leads that person to a conclusion. This should surely be the expectation of the correspondent also. After all, if you ask a stranger to advise you what to do about a situation, then you are giving them permission to tell you what they think you need (not necessarily want) to hear. That's the bargain you enter into when you divulge all to an agony columnist.

Let's look at a couple of examples. I want them to be real examples—situations that correspondents have sent to columnists and have been answered in actual newspapers and magazines, but I am going to paraphrase the letters so as not to plagiarise or reproduce printed material.

Here's part of a letter from a woman who signs herself "Guilty", as quite a lot of correspondents do.

My husband's mother has always been a joy to know and highly supportive of me. Now she has developed dementia and the assumption is that she will move in to our home and that I shall be expected to do nearly all the caring since my husband still works full-time. There has been no explicit discussion of this. Now that my children have grown-up and left home, I was looking forward to doing the things I wanted to do. I feel terribly guilty for thinking like this, but I really dread the prospect of having to be a full-time carer. Can you offer any solutions?

You'll recall the decision that Emma and her husband had to make; this one has some similarities with it but is not the same.

I'll try to bullet-point the response from the columnist/columnists to whom the letter was sent:

- You are wonderful for your loving, caring response to the situation, doubts and dreads and all.

- You have not been trained or prepared for a job which is extremely challenging, so you have every right to feel alarmed.

- There is no real solution to your situation.

- What you can do is to take action. Get busy finding out about all the support you can draw on, including the organisations that specialise in dementia care and all the services local to you.

- Once you know where your support is coming from, you can draw up support rotas which should also include your husband (and children?)

- Model yourself as a competent but far from exclusive carer. Don't allow resentment to eat away at you because it will also show in all you do. Do make sure your own needs are catered for.

- Seek therapy and involve your husband in this. This will help you to maintain boundaries and communicate openly and honestly.

So what might the Killer Question be that would most help "Guilty" to move forward? What might the columnist(s) suggest above and beyond the (doubtless) highly empathic and helpful comments they have already proffered?

The problem for any columnist is not so much that they don't have a grip on the situation: the letters they receive are often much more detailed than the stripped-down printed versions. The real problem is that they will not know how their response is received (unless the correspondent gets back to them). So any Killer Question they suggest might not quite hit the mark, or miss it completely.

It's a stab in the light, but not necessarily experienced as the right stab. As I've indicated plenty of times already, the discovery of the Killer Question is often a process of trial and error involving a lot of minor tweaking or "back to the drawing board" when that doesn't work. There are frequently several iterations before the "Ha, ha" moment of formulating exactly the right one. That's why it's so valuable to work out the Killer Question with the person concerned, ideally face-to-face but through Zoom, Facetime, Skype or similar if not.

So regard the following suggestions as stabs in the light. We know at least the gist of the situation (so we're not in the dark) but we don't know if the stab will hit the right target.

> Q. *What action do I need to take to turn dread into calm acceptance of having mum-in-law stay with us?*

> Q. *Would I feel relatively happy (and certainly not dread) if I can secure a support network for my mum-in-law so that I become one carer among many?*

> Q. *Can I imagine getting to the point where I can timetable a support programme for mum-in-law and a "me time" one for myself that will leave me both guilt-free and dread-free?*

I have no firm idea whether any of these questions would be spot on for "Guilty", but I think they offer similar but different possibilities. The first one is at the most general level and presupposes the *fait accompli* nature of the situation. All three suggest action as the key to "solving" the situation and turn on the reassuring idea (that could become fact) that "you are not alone". Two and three invite the correspondent to imagine people and services that could help her out. Three offers the most specific visualisation of the "solution" in the form of timetables. It's quite likely that different individuals would prefer different questions. Perhaps "Guilty" could be offered all three as variants of the same idea and let her choose her favourite.

Let's consider a second situation addressed by an agony columnist. I'll try to summarise the letter s/he has received.

I haven't seen one of my sisters for more than three decades. I had little to do with her when we were growing up and many of her behaviours, including her aggression, were challenging. She did herself no favours at the funeral of one of our parents and didn't bother attending the funeral of the other. The problem is that she has recently died and one of her son's has invited me to attend the funeral and assist with the costs. What do you suggest?

The columnist's remarks and suggestions—all spot on, I think—can be summarised as follows:

- We often have to attend funerals of people we don't particularly like or even know.

- Turn up with good grace and try to find good things to say about your sister.

- Don't hold your sister's child responsible for your sibling's behaviour.

- Contribute to the funeral costs as requested.

- Seize this as a chance to show generosity of spirit.

The possible Killer Questions are not difficult to fathom. Contenders include:

Q. Would I really present as a generous and warm-hearted person if I refused my nephew's requests?

Q. Would I like the person I'll come across as if I refuse my nephew's requests?

Q. Could responding positively to my nephew's letter offer several opportunities?

or

Q. Could responding positively to my nephew's letter offer several opportunities—coming across well, feeling good about myself, having graceful closure with a sister I was alienated from, and perhaps developing a relationship with a nephew I've never met?

Once again, notice that these questions follow much the same theme but with tweaks that make them significantly different. Unless we know the correspondent and, in particular, what most matters to them (e.g. reputation with others? reputation with self?) it's almost impossible to know which, if any of these questions, they'd want to decide upon. Perhaps they'd be happy with any one of the three/four. In a face-to-face coaching session it would be possible to formulate the Killer Question with the active participation of the individual so their preference would be obvious.

Notice that the fourth question is an expanded version of the third. Which is better? My preference is for the short form because it requires more from the individual concerned. More of the ball is in their court, and it's up to them to think about the specific opportunities that going to the funeral and helping with the costs might bring. Eliciting those is possible in the coaching context but not so easy in the agony aunt/uncle context when the communication is a fixed exchange: one writes, the other responds.

Coaches

Life coaches and other types of coach are similar to agony columnists in that they too are in helping relationships. If you have a troublesome decision to be made, then you might feel that either type of helper could be useful to you. However, coaches tend to relate to their clients differently from the way agony columnists relate to their correspondents. The former are likely to want to elicit more of the solutions from their clients and to try to avoid rescuing them—doing for them what they can and should do for themselves. Why? Because rescuing is usually disrespectful, since it implies that the other person lacks the nous or wherewithal to come to their own conclusions. In practice this means that coaches are likely to ask questions more than make assertions, offer advice or provide prescriptions. Agony columnists may also want to respect the capacities of their correspondent, but usually won't be able to truly interact with them, certainly not through a face-to-face exchange, so the flow is more one way. This inevitably means more emphasis on suggestions and advice. That's fine, because that's what those who seek them know they are going to get.

Much depends on the precise circumstances, but a good

coach is more likely to help the client tease out their own Killer Question than to suggest a question for them to address. They might put it in very general terms to begin with:

Which question might best help you decide which path to take?

And then, depending on the client's capacity to do this unaided and their level of certainty that they had formulated the right question, would pose other clarifying questions as required. For example:

You've used "I" rather than "we". Does that feel like the right word to use—and, of course, it may be?

You're asking yourself whether you find your job "rewarding" enough to stay in it. Does "rewarding" feel like the word that will best let you know what decision to make? Do you want to try out some other words to test their impact?

If the client says "yes" and asks for suggestions, then the coach can either come back with his/her own suggestions or put the ball back in the client's court and ask him/her to make some.

Does my job "thrill me", or does it "get me up in the morning", or does it "give me a strong sense of fulfilment", or "does it provide me with the kinds of challenges I want".

The client might decide that "rewarding" is still the best fit, might decide that one of the coach's suggestions hits the mark, or might sense that s/he still hasn't quite found the words that will enable them to decide confidently one way or the other.

As I've indicated, formulating just the right Killer Question can take time, experimentation, winnowing, substitution, testing and, sometimes, scrapping the original question altogether and starting from scratch. The process is pretty much the same whether you are doing it alone and unaided or whether someone else is seeking to assist you. Certainly, a skilful coach can be a blessing, especially for someone who has been trying to work out how to make a tough decision and has managed only to get themselves increasingly confused.

Chapter 7

Killer Questions in the public realm

Because the emphasis in this book is on personal decision-making for individuals, couples and families, most of the case studies and examples are similarly personal and inter-personal in kind. But Killer Questions are just as relevant to the public sphere as they are to the personal. Indeed, because the decisions themselves can impact on the lives of a great many people, lots of them are even more significant. So I am going to devote a bit of space to decisions that governments, public bodies, companies and all kinds of other organisations have to make, and you yourself might be involved in making if you are connected with them.

I'm convinced that seeking a Killer Question to make a difficult decision is as valid and vital for, say, a corporation as it is for a couple. But I'm aware that there are differences and challenges. The chief of these is that corporations, councils, charities and other public organisations are expected to be accountable for the decisions they make. This might require them to explain the thinking behind them and to "show their working out". Very often they will need to demonstrate that they have taken a range of considerations and viewpoints into account, which might mean that they automatically default to a balance model. They might default to that model because that's just what they are used to working with.

If it's misunderstood, or used illegitimately, then the use of the Killer Question could seem dodgy. It could appear to be reductionist, over-simplifying a complex issue. It might also come across as a "stitch-up", pushing or even predetermining a particular outcome. If so, it certainly won't be universally well-received.

By way of example, take the current debate about whether more roads should be given over exclusively to pedestrians and cyclists. Some residents and road-users of targeted streets are in favour of this; others are not, arguing that it penalises car drivers and prevents ambulances, police cars and fire engines responding to emergencies efficiently. Suppose a local council, minded to pedestrianise a residential street, sought a Killer Question to help them determine their policy and seek public support for it. Suppose it decided on the following question:

How can we pedestrianise the road without inconveniencing the emergency services?

Would this gain acceptance? It might if the decision to close the road to vehicular traffic had been taken and was no longer up for discussion. If that were not the case, and the council purported to be in consultation stage, then I think most residents would feel peeved. They'd rightly conclude that the question presupposed that the road would be closed to traffic other than emergency service vehicles.

The problem is not with the principle of the Killer Question. The problem is with its formulation. Here are two versions that might garner wider support if nothing had genuinely been settled about possible changes to road use:

How can we make the road more pedestrian-friendly whilst causing minimal inconvenience to the emergency services and the road's car users?

How can we prevent the road being used as a busy and dangerous cut-through for traffic without inconveniencing the residents or the emergency services?

I'm not suggesting that any of the formulations are ideal or the obvious go-to version. Neither am I suggesting that it's possible to come up with a form of words that pleases everybody. But what these questions demonstrate, I hope, is that it is entirely possible, appropriate and, I'd argue, mightily helpful, to decide on the question that would best facilitate the making of the decision itself.

It would seem to me more helpful to have a question that accurately reflects the core of the issue and so gains the general support of those being consulted, than either to present a bald question with a binary response ("Are you in favour of pedestrianising ___ Road?") or else making a policy decision ("The Council is intending to pedestrianise ___ Road") and solicit responses to it. To my mind, the Killer Questions stands more chance of engaging the residents and less likely to put their backs up because it suggests that the Council is trying to be as accommodating and responsive as possible.

Let me give one other example of use of the Killer question

for making non-personal decisions, in this case, one that's affecting millions.

During the coronavirus pandemic, the UK government, like governments around the world, had to make many very difficult decisions, often with limited information and often knowing that their decisions would upset many of their citizens. One of the more difficult decision the UK government had to make was whether or not to have a second national lockdown in (mainly) November 2020.

Of course, I wasn't party to the deliberations that Boris Johnson had with his ministerial colleagues and his top scientific advisers, but I'd be willing to bet that their strategy involved weighing up the pros and cons. As you know by now, this is what almost everyone and every organisation does when faced with a difficult decision, usually a stark binary choice. It's probably what most of us think Boris et al *should* have done. Indeed, when talking about responses to Covid-19, many commentators have spoken about "getting the balance right". They were referring to the balance between (to put it crudely) lives and livelihoods, but it's the image of the balance we're interested in here.

It all seems so reasonable, so obvious. But you'll know by now that the time I've spent helping struggling decision-makers has shown me how tiresomely unproductive it can be. And you will know the main reason for this: using a weighing strategy means see-sawing with the arguments for and the arguments against. The see-saw rarely comes to a firm and definite rest, rarely brings you to a conclusion you can trust. It's always possible to come up with more arguments (including more data) one way or another, or to weight them differently, and then off it goes again. Perpetual uncertainty is almost factored into the process. If a decision is made, then it's often made with little conviction or even made randomly.

I suspect this is how the Prime Minister came to the decision he did: with huge ambivalence but tilting to the view that the pros of a second lockdown outweighed the cons of doing so. But I also bet that the timescale on which the balancing deliberations were based was a short one—probably the two months to Christmas.

How might it have been done differently? And how might a different decision have been reached? The answer, I believe, lies in finding the Killer Question. This strategy is likely to include some consideration of the pros and cons, but the objective is to strip away those that will probably not swing the decision one way or another and, ultimately, to formulate the Killer Question that will determine the decision. If it's the right Killer Question, then it will get to the heart of the matter. It doesn't need to be complex or profound, though it might be.

What might the Killer Question have been had Boris Johnson and his team sought to identify it?

Bearing in mind also what I've said about the best decisions being those that focus primarily on long-term interests, then this is a likely formulation:

What do we want the country to be like by the end of 2021?

The "be like" would need some discussion and detailing. It would include some thinking about the numbers of people who had died from Covid-19 and the state of the NHS. But it would undoubtedly prioritise the state of the economy, the health of the whole business sector, employment levels, the state of the arts, the mental health of the country's citizens, and so on. Would the decision-makers have decided that a lockdown would best serve these longer term interests, especially if they also (secretly?) believed that the lockdown would probably "need" to be extended and/or repeated? I somehow doubt it.

I'm sure many people who had not read the book you are holding would contend that you can't make a massively consequential decision on the basis of one straightforward question. The situation, they'd say, is far too complex for that. I'd respond by suggesting that a straightforward question is precisely what the PM was haunted by as he and his co-conspirators were weighing up the pros and cons, except that the question in his head was: "What do we want the country to be like in the run up to Christmas?" In other words, the decision to lockdown was made on the basis of a different Killer Question and, arguably, the wrong one. That's my conclusion, of course; yours may be different.

I can think of an alternative Killer Question that might also have provided a steer for decision-making. It's this:

What phrase best sums up what the coronavirus pandemic represents and also helps us make the right decisions for responding to it?

One possible answer would have been: "It's a manageable menace". The goal might have been to modulate this into "a manageable nuisance". The "manageable" qualifier would emphasise agency and avoid prescriptions that were overly fear-driven. Most hospitality settings would have argued that this is precisely how they had regarded Covid-19—as a challenge they could handle through careful regulation. "Manageable" also hints at a situation that is not going away any time soon, so best treated as enduring or even endemic.

The starting point is different, but I suspect that this Killer Question would lead to the same decision and the same consequential action as the one above: no lockdown, just an end-directed, ongoing set of stringently applied measures with the minimal necessary impact on livelihoods, and as much as realistically possible, on lives as well.

You may not agree with much of this, and it's not my intention to suggest that I know best. But I do hope you at least buy into the decision-making power and value of Killer Questions—even for major decisions that affect us all as well as those that only impact us personally.

Chapter 8

A simple, crazy way to get conviction

There's another way to make a fork-in-the-road decision. On the face of it, it seems crazy, but experience suggests to me that it's almost a sure-fire way to know if you've got the right response to your Killer Question. That way is to **toss a coin.**

Your immediate, visceral response to tossing a coin can give you the kind of conviction it's hard to get in any other way. But to be as sure as you can be of making the right decision (i) there's a condition that has to be met, and (ii) there is a way of knowing that is absolutely crucial.

First the condition. Tossing a coin to make a scary "Should I or Shouldn't I?" decision only works if your mind-body already knows what your response needs to be. At a conscious level you may still be torn, but at a sub-conscious level, or in the most aware parts of your being, the response that is in your best interests is probably already known. If you toss a coin, then you might need at least a dim awareness of this—a sense that this is so.

We've spoken already about your mind-body's distributed intelligence, and how your heart, your gut, your nervous system and the thinking cells of your body have profound intelligence about what is right for you. Your mind alone is not always as smart; you can use your brain to self-deceive or over-ride your better instincts. If your brain is working in tandem with the rest of you, then you have an optimal internal guidance system. But even if it isn't, your bodily intelligence can alert you to what is in line with your best interests.

This can happen when you toss a coin. But here's the crucial point: **what matters is not the side the coin falls down on but your immediate bodily response to it.** It's your reaction that indicates what you decision should be, not whether it's heads for one choice or tails for the other. This is what I'm referring to when I talk of an absolutely crucial way of knowing.

I'm going to illustrate this process with an actual example.

Many years ago, a middle-aged man called Ron had a well-paid and highly responsible job, but the organisation he worked for had a restructuring and he was invited to apply for another position. He'd already been through four other restructures. Each time he'd been fortunate not only to secure another job but a better one. But this time he was torn between going through the whole re-appointment process or taking a step into the unknown and setting up in business by himself. The latter option had been gnawing at him for some time.

Here's the crucial bit. The first step in the process was an assessment centre held in a hotel. When he drove into the car park of the hotel at 8.15 in the morning he still hadn't made his fork-in-the-road decision. He had just minutes to do so. So he decided to toss a coin: heads for stay, tails for go. The coin came down on the heads side. But Ron knew immediately from the wrench in his stomach that this was not the right decision for him. His gut was telling him something he couldn't ignore or silence. He accepted that message and immediately went into the hotel and told the HR personnel that he was not going to go through with the assessment centre because he was intending to leave. They tried to persuade him to think again, but he knew the visceral reaction was absolutely trustworthy. His gut knew best.

Ron believed that timing played a part. Had he tossed a coin, say, weeks before the re-appointment process started, he wasn't at all certain that he would have experienced the same undeniable reaction. But right up against it time-wise, in a now-or-never moment, the reaction came.

(Incidentally, Ron never regretted the choice he made, and came to realise that this was one of the most significant moments of his life. It had provided him with an immeasurably powerful reference experience.)

Throughout this book I've used the word "response" to denote what our mind or mind-body does and feels about something. "Response" usually suggests some degree of conscious awareness and agency. But when it comes to coin tossing, the word "reaction" is spot on. It captures the non-conscious immediacy of the feedback we get from our mind-body intelligence. It's in the driving seat and all we do is provide the stimulus: in this instance, the toss of a coin that triggers an answer.

Should you really decide your future on the toss of a coin? Most people would shudder at the idea. It seems too random and wouldn't be informed by your principal considerations, or by any at all. But there are three arguments for choosing one of two paths based on the toss of a coin. One is that we are enlisting the help of a source of wisdom beyond our own: fate, destiny, the universe, God—name it as you will—is deciding for you. This takes a huge dollop of faith in an invisible force. Most of us probably wouldn't assume that this produces the best result. Chances are, though, that we've already rehearsed the arguments endlessly in our head and done our homework, so in tossing a coin we are simply enlisting an additional but qualitatively different source of wisdom.

The second argument has more going for it: it's the view that what most matters is making the decision **work** rather than the decision itself. If it's a close and balanced call, then why not let a coin decide and then commit 100% to implementing it. After all, at the time of making a big decision, we rarely have anything like enough information to know for certain how things will turn out. Putting everything we have into making whatever decision we've made work at least puts us in the driving seat.

Arguably, almost any decision can be made to work if you put enough into making it work… madness can be put to rest when you refuse to think too much about the path you didn't choose.

Third, as I've already argued, our mind-body often knows best. If we allow it to interpret the coin-toss result then it will guide us in the right direction. If we regard it as a more reliable source of wisdom than, say, fate, then we will let it take priority over fate. If the coin falls on the "wrong" side for us, then a strong internal reaction will tell us to ignore it and go with our gut. That's how it worked for Ron on the cusp of a major career decision. But as I've indicated before, it only works for personal decisions in which your bodily intelligence can be informative. Don't go tossing a coin to tell you whether to bet on your football club winning or losing. Your bodily intelligence is unlikely to be of much help.

If at the heart of our being we know what is right for us, then our gut or heart will let us know. At least, that has been my experience and there's a lot of neuro-cardiological evidence to support it[3]. I appreciate that some people may take a lot of convincing.

Chapter 9

Not completely convinced?

Having ventured this far with the book, I trust you are at least 90% persuaded by my principal argument: that the way to make a big, scary decision is to focus primarily on the most significant determinant, to formulate this as what I call the Killer Question and to make your decision based on your response to it.

It's possible that you might have one or two lingering doubts, qualms or questions. I might not be able to allay or answer them all, but I want to make a stab at anticipating and addressing them.

Q1. Surely, many situations where big decisions have to be taken are messy and multi-factorial. There are many things that need to be considered and you can't reduce complex reality into one issue, important as it may be.

That's a fair point, and I have some sympathy with it. I'm going to offer some thoughts to ponder without denying that the objection has some validity.

First, many of the people I've sought to help have been more than aware of the messiness and complexity of their situations, and that's what's bogged them down. They've tried to honour rather than mask that complexity, but with the result that they've been befuddled by everything they've tried to consider. Not being able to see the wood for the trees is frustrating and debilitating. What we need to work with is manageable complexity.

Whenever we try to represent or model some aspect of reality—in a map, for example, or a model of, say, a river valley or the human nervous system—we have to make its complexity manageable. Some degree of simplification is required, otherwise it has little value. If we try to put everything in then the critical elements get lost. And we do too.

That's also what we need to do with decision-making situations. I acknowledge this in the sections of the book that deal with the balance approach and weighting. We can get overwhelmed with details if we identify zillions of pros and cons but don't prioritise them, don't focus on the critical few and don't bracket off those that won't make a difference to the final decision. This can be preparatory to the approach I advocate.

I've never worked with anybody where all the factors were of equal significance. There are always hierarchies of significance and these both reflect and order the complexity. Some things matter more than others, and helping those concerned to work out which ones matter the most is key to decision coaching. Individuals are often good at identifying arguments for and against, but less good at grasping their relative significance, and less good still at identifying the absolutely critical few or one that will make all the difference to their final decision.

Here's another thought. We might contend that the reality of a situation is too complex for decisions to be determined by a few critical considerations. But if decisions were determined by a few critical considerations, then perhaps that reality would present as a lot less complex.

Q2. On the same theme, wouldn't the complexity of a situation be better captured by a series of questions or tests rather than by just one Killer Question?

This is certainly an alternative and valid approach to decision-making. Indeed, it's the approach some other writers have taken; for example, Mira Kirshenbaum in her admirable book **Too Good to Leave, Too Bad to Stay** (see end-note ii). There is an element of this in my approach in that I speak about the critical few (factors). I point out, with examples, that a linked pair of questions is sometimes required and I encourage a move from pros and cons thinking to devising test questions or conditions that need to be met.

A battery of test questions works better when focussing solely and comprehensively on a single subject area. For instance, Kirshenbaum's book deals exclusively with (largely) long-term relationships. Her test questions map the territory she is dealing with and highlight a range of issues common to committed relationships generally. The reader can engage with those most relevant to them. I did much the same thing with and for a client trying to decide whether she should stay friends with a man she really liked or attempt to become much more than just friends. A menu of off-the-shelf questions from which users can pick and choose undoubtedly has appeal.

My book is not subject-specific but rather about big, scary decisions of all sorts, so menus of questions are much less appropriate. Also, my experience is that bespoke questions are more appropriate and more powerful than multiple-choice options proffered by someone else, even if that person is an expert in the relevant area. This is especially the case if the decision-maker has identified and crafted them, probably after other questions have been contemplated and rejected as just not critical and determining enough.

Perhaps the Killer Question approach sacrifices quantity to quality, but in the end it's the quality of the question that matters. I contend that one question can do most if not all of the heavy-lifting if it captures the heart, apex or most critical dimension of the decision-making situation. This harks back to the hierarchy of the significance idea. Almost always the pros and cons or the factors to be considered are arranged hierarchically. Think of a triangle with levels. The higher the level the more important the factors are and, generally, the fewer they are. My approach is focussed on the apex because that's where the critical few factors are located and, especially, the most critical factor of all. Since the decision turns on the decision-maker's response to the question that pivots on this, it's rightly the focus of most attention.

Here's another interesting observation I dealt with earlier: When problems are arranged hierarchically, solve the highest level problem and there's a strong possibility of resolving or dissolving many of the lower level problems. Either they get sorted or they are no longer relevant or active. The implication is that if problems are connected or entangled in this way, then they don't need to be picked off separately one at a time. The whole job can be done by tackling the problem at the top. It's smart and very efficient.

I'm not suggesting that all the factors relevant to making a big, difficult decision are connected, causally or otherwise, but the Killer Question method can sometimes serve to clear up a range of other issues. Often when people decide to make a big change in their lives, such as re-committing fully to a partner they were having doubts about, leaving a job they were dissatisfied with or coming out about their gender preferences, a whole bunch of the difficulties they had been experiencing cease to exist or matter. I'd be very surprised if you couldn't think of your own experiences of this.

So: should we make a decision based on several factors or on one overriding factor? In the end, it's a choice and there are arguments for both. The Killer Question method doesn't have to be followed to the absolute letter; you can combine it with other questions or tests if you like (see Q.3). But experience convinces me that there is no more potent way to make up one's mind than identifying the Killer Question. It has something to do with the power and satisfaction of crystallisation, something to do with the profound simplicity we can find when we see beyond the seeming complexity of a situation, something to do with capturing the whole in the part, especially when that part does much to sum up the whole, and something to do with the laser-like focus we bring to bear once we've formulated the Killer Question.

Trying to decide on the basis of several questions is like switching on a number of normal lightbulbs each radiating a bit of light adding up to lots of small but merged pools of illumination. Deciding on the basis of a Killer Question is like using the focussed, brilliant intensity of a laser beam. You get more concentrated illumination.

Dispersed illumination or focussed? It's a choice.

Q3. You allude a lot in the book to tests, as well as in your answer above, but you don't devote a specific section to using a battery of tests or tick-box strategy to make big decisions.

As I hope I've made clear, making big decisions is best done using the kind of diagnostic thinking used by doctors and other professionals (e.g. electrical engineers) who use tests to arrive at conclusion-type decisions. The Killer Question is a kind of ultimate and all-determining test. I allude to decision-making tools that are, in effect, a list of tests and conditions: the person specification used to select job candidates is an example. I don't devote much time specifically to the tick-box strategy for making decisions; I focus more on the pros and cons approach because it's the way most people try to decide about big, scary issues. But I acknowledge that ticking boxes (ie setting conditions to be met) is a decision-making strategy, and something of a half-way house between the balance approach and the Killer Question approach.

Like the balance approach, the emphasis is on listing things to consider, not this time in the form of pros and cons but rather on the "must haves" and (sometimes but not always) "must not haves". Like the Killer Question strategy, the emphasis is on diagnostic testing. Sometimes the pros and cons approach is used for the main decision and the tick-box approach is used to proceed. For example, I've known lots of people decide to move house after using the balance method and then chosen their actual house using the tick-box approach. But I've also known people who have used the tick-box approach decide in favour of a house that received precious few ticks.

I'm aware, though, that tick-box thinking is the default method by which some people seek to make decisions about big matters. One of its virtues is that it requires those drawing them up to be as clear as possible about their criteria or conditions. This can also be its major drawback. Why? Because tick lists can be clung to inflexibly, misconceived in the first place and irrelevant to the final decision.

I've known people throw their tick list out of the window when they've made a choice that goes against virtually everything they thought they were looking for. The partner they choose has qualities not on the tick-list and lacks some that are. On TV programmes about property seekers, such as Escape to the Country, it's not unusual to encounter someone who thinks they want a four-bedroom house with a large garden and then fall in love with a three-bedroom cottage with a tiny back-yard! For me, a tick list is a tool for guidance, and one to hold on to lightly, not a full-proof strategy to be followed slavishly in the kinds of decision-making situations this book is concerned with.

Using a tick-list, you can end up with ticks against each box and yet still not come to a decision with conviction. Some job candidates meet all the criteria on a person specification but the members of the selection panel have an intuition or a gut feeling telling them that to appoint these people would be a mistake. My own experience of being on job selection panels tells me just this: ignore gut feelings at your peril (even if it makes Human Resources uneasy!).

Using a tick list, you may not be frustrated with the see-sawing ambivalence you get with the balance approach, but it can still be hard to exit with confidence. You march step by step towards a definite conclusion, but end up dissatisfied with the destination. Not always, of course, but quite often. Also, if only some boxes are ticked, then you have to decide the significance of those not met. Were the "must haves" not that must have after all?

In short, my view is this: a tick-box approach to making big personal decisions can yield better results than a pros and cons approach but it's nowhere near as good as using a Killer Question or two. The latter gets you to the nub of the situation in a way that tick-boxing doesn't. It may sound counter-intuitive, but results are often more convincing when you put your whole focus on one all-important, all-determining, sign-posting test question than when you put it on many moderately important ones. Back to my light bulb *v* laser image of illumination.

Actually, in practice, the tick box approach can and often does feed into the Killer Question strategy just as the balance approach can. That is, the two approaches are not mutually exclusive. We start by identifying the tick-boxes or conditions and out of these deliberations the Killer Question emerges or is fashioned. The Killer Question might represent a highly condensed version of the more critical conditions. Or while it might appear to hang there in splendid isolation, there are supplementary questions linked to particular bits of it, perhaps annotated if the Killer Question is written down. Let's illustrate this.

Amanda's dilemma

Amanda is a married woman in her 40s. She's come to the view that she and her husband are just ill-matched. She's spoken to him on various occasions about what he needs to do to convince her otherwise. He's made some attempts to do this, but hasn't sustained them or convinced his wife that he has the capacity to change. She also feels guilty about asking him to change radically because she feels it's selfish, knows her husband is fundamentally a good man and knows that she has to make changes herself. She's spent a lot of time deciding the conditions that would need to be met for her to stay with her husband. You will see that the Killer Question she is now working with is a kind of imploded version or summary of her thinking about the specific conditions she needs to be met. (See below)

Amanda's Killer Question and her annotations of it:

> I need to know the timescale will be as short as realistically possible

> I need to be convinced he has the capacity as well as the motivation to change radically

Is Craig <u>ever</u> going to be <u>able</u> to <u>change enough</u> for me to feel convinced that he's <u>the right life partner</u> for me?

- Move from a minimal doer to a full partner role

- Really be present with me when we talk

- Change his default brusqueness

- Be whatever it takes (I'm not sure what) for there to be chemistry between us

- Convince me that he's moved from a "me" to "us" way of thinking and doing

- Convince me that he's really up for doing things together

Amanda has decided that the answer is very probably "no" but owes it to her husband, their relationship and the children to give him the opportunity to demonstrate otherwise. The situation is on-going, but what is certain is that Amanda is absolutely certain that she has finally formulated exactly the right Killer Question for the situation she is in. There were plenty of previous, not-quite-right iterations.

Q4. *You say that when people make big decisions they aren't swayed by minor considerations, by pros or cons that they give low scores to. But don't minor considerations sometimes make a big difference to how people decide? Also, don't a lot of minor pros or cons sometimes tip the balance away from some bigger factor?*

People are quite often swayed by minor considerations, though what counts as "minor" isn't always clear and obvious and is often a very personal matter. For example, I once worked with a businessman who decided to locate his new premises close to the golf course of which his (persuasive, much younger) wife was a member. That was his primary consideration, and most people would think that was a pretty minor one. I also recall a woman whose main reason for wanting to leave her husband (or the main reason she gave) was his constant whistling. (She was especially irritated by the fact that his whistling was random and he never whistled "proper tunes".) I don't know if she did leave her husband and whether it was mainly because of his whistling habit. I do know that the businessman regretted his location decision.

So here's the point: just because minor pros or cons can skew our decision-making, it doesn't mean that they should. It's usually a source of regret if we let them. Helping someone appreciate this can be a key bit of decision coaching. Sometimes it involves teasing out the private logic behind what seems to be an over-representation of something that looks unimportant. The truth is, we don't always know how significant a factor is to us, or why we accord it the significance we do. That's why the process of weighting and scoring pros and cons is important and sometimes illuminating, even if it doesn't allow us to finish the decision-making job satisfactorily.

The key point is that if we come to accept that a reason for acting one way or another is not important, or not important to us, then it makes no sense for it to exert undue influence on the decision we make. If something seems minor to other people but is truly major to us, then it can legitimately kick above its weight when it comes to deciding. An incessant whistling habit might be one such consideration. But in truth, I'd want to delve a bit deeper rather than accept it at face-value.

Helping someone really understand just how significant something is to them can be a crucial contribution to the quality of their decision-making. Ditching further consideration of matters that are not going to influence the "Should I, Shouldn't I?" decision is a critical bit of the deliberation process. It's clearing the decks to allow attention to focus on what really is going to affect the decision.

I wonder, also, whether according prominence to seemingly minor or even trivial factors is something more of us do nowadays than we did in the past. What I call the dynamics of disproportionality is much in evidence; on social media, for example, where a lot of people seem to over-react, take offence at almost any small comment they disagree with and make huge mountains out of very small mole-hills. If I'm right, then it's possible that learning how to make decisions based on identifying what really matters, what is really important in the grand scheme of things, will be a big piece of personal development.

A sense of proportionality tends to be a feature of good decision-making. Over-reacting to minor considerations or, indeed, under-reacting to major ones, is likely to result in decisions that don't work out well long-term. It's rather like what happens when our immune system reacts excessively to something harmless (a peanut) or reacts inadequately to something harmful (a flu virus). Both result in illness.

Becoming more wise and more mature has a lot to do with becoming increasingly better at distinguishing the importance of things. Given this, questing for Killer Questions amounts to questing for greater wisdom or, to put it more colloquially, to becoming increasingly better at sorting the wheat from the chaff.

As for the contention that a lot of minor pros and cons could collectively out-weigh the influence of the critical few or critical one, again, in reality, this sometimes is the case. I've certainly worked with people who've cobbled together all manner of minor pros in order to "justify" staying in a job or house or with a partner and sought to down-play the significant cons. The question is whether this is good decision-making and whether it leads to outcomes that are in the best interests of those involved. My experience is that it rarely is. More often than not, individuals who keep referring to minor considerations, those they know are minor but are inflating their significance, are often trying to convince themselves to decide in the wrong direction. Often it's in order to take the easier path, even though it's unlikely to be the right one in the longer term.

Just as no wrong can make a right, no collection of small considerations can accumulate enough "rightness" to justify a wrong decision. Or, more accurately, an optimal decision. In reality, a lot of people do settle for a decision they know is not ideal or optimal. They may see little option. They may think of it as a "realistic" accommodation. They may do it from a sense of duty or because they don't want to hurt other people. I've known people to stay in marriages and jobs they don't want to be in for those kinds of reasons. I'm not condemning decisions like these, but this book has been written to guide people into making big, scary decisions that are as optimal as possible. Nearly always that means privileging the most critical factors, not trying to bury them beneath a mound of trivial ones.

Q5. The circumstances people find themselves in can be very limiting or difficult to do anything about, and the Killer Question approach might seem to under-estimate these. It's all very well saying that the Killer Question will tell you what decision to make, but in reality things aren't this simple. You might know what you'd like to do but for various reasons to do with circumstances or practicalities it's just not possible to do them.

The Killer Question is not a passport to the ideal future. It's designed to help you know what your decision should be. It won't in itself magic away the implementation challenges. The Killer Question strategy assumes that the individuals concerned have some degree of agency that allows them to act rather than just allowing circumstances to act upon them. But it doesn't presuppose complete autonomy. There may well be things they can do little about, at least at the present time.

Mary didn't have the wherewithal to leave the marital home as soon as she decided that leaving was the right choice for her. One of her concerns was to try to ensure that her husband would fare well enough after she had left, so she put in a lot of time and effort into that. She also decided she needed to put money aside for her future, and that delayed her departure. There were all manner of other practical matters she wanted to sort before she left, so her Killer Question didn't usher in a stress-free future, certainly not immediately.

What I have found is that identifying the core issue and expressing it as a Killer Question can be in itself empowering and energising. Once someone is clear about the path ahead and convinced that it's the right one, they can become very resourceful. They find ways of negotiating the hurdles that previously seemed insurmountable. An emphatic Killer Question response can elicit a new lease of life. Messy, real-world complications don't disappear but there's renewed energy to tackle them. Indeed, if there is not a sense of renewed energy and determination, then that's an indication that the person might not have found the real Killer Question. A tell-tale sign for me is a lot of "Yes, buts". "Yes, I know what I should do, but what about X, Y and Z?" These aren't encouraging signs.

There won't be many individuals who don't have some practical concerns or even a few doubts about how realistic it is to follow their chosen path. That's understandable. But if they have conviction and a degree of agency, then chances are they will see ways around the difficulties in their way.

People who lack agency are unlikely ever to get to a Killer Question, let alone commit to its outcomes. They will make all kinds of excuses along the way. Negative and cynical people likewise. This book is not intended for them and I rarely work with such people. Their attitudes are draining, and I decided long ago that you can't help someone make a decision if they are unwilling to do more for themselves than you are for them.

Q6. *You don't have much truck with the balance method of decision-making, and I accept your reasons why, but it has worked for me on occasions.*

Then by all means use it. The truth is, we nearly all use it, or some version of it, for many of the everyday decisions we make. We tot up the pros and cons of, say, shopping on-line as opposed to going to the supermarket, and if we are reasonably happy with what we decide, then we go with it. If we're happy enough with what we've decided, then fine. Seeking the Killer Question might seem unnecessary, though I have to admit that I've got into the habit of doing so for even moderately significant decisions. For this one, for example, I'd probably ask myself: "Are the gains I'll get from going to the supermarket great enough to warrant the time I'll have to give to something I don't like doing?" For me, it's just a snappier and clarifying way of arranging the pros and cons. To use the terminology I used earlier, it's a more efficient recipe or strategy to reach the same outcome.

I am also convinced that the balance method has the inherent limitations I've discussed: above all, how difficult it can be to get to a point of certainty and decisiveness. So many of the people I've worked with have spoken about "going around in circles", or something similar, trying to make their mind up about something really important. Not being able to exit the deliberation stage is extremely frustrating, and that's why I've tried to help people to do just that by finding the crucial test question that brings deliberation to a close. The Killer Question strategy may not be your default, go-to strategy for making choices, but on the occasions when the balance method gets you nowhere, it is the option I would take.

Of course, if you have a different strategy that works well for you, then use that.

There's a horses-for-courses point to make here.

What I have observed in many years of training and coaching people to make better decisions (or, more accurately, to better make decisions) is that the balance method seems to work better for people with certain traits. Individuals who are very methodical, often "process", and procedural people who like to use lists of tick-boxes or spread-sheets to work towards a decision, tend to fare better with a pros and cons approach. I don't mean this in any way disrespectfully, but individuals on the ASD spectrum, at the milder Aspergers end, often seem comfortable making decisions in a rational, tick-box and points scoring way. Faith in the quantitative approach ("the scores will tell me how to decide") appears to provide the reassurance some people seek.

Q7. You place a lot of emphasis upon the sensations you get from your body as well as your mind when making decisions. What if I don't seem to get these feelings?

The kinds of big, scary decisions this book is about do have an emotional (better still, psycho-emotional) dimension, usually a very major one. The decisions are personal ones but likely to affect other people. Some decisions have less of an emotional component or, arguably, none at all: decisions about where to site gas pipes or about bus time-tables, for instance. They may have emotional ramifications (people can get heated about them) but those making them may not need to "go inside" and work out what their body thinks about them. Indeed, they may be settled by rule books, regulation manuals, algorithms or mathematical models. I'm assuming this is not the case for the decisions challenging readers of this book, at least, not in their personal lives.

Yes, I do place a lot of importance on the signals we get from what I call the mind-body (because the mind and body are best thought about as an integrated whole even if they don't always work that way). We are designed to get signals of comfort and discomfort from our physiology as well as our brains. Crudely put, these help us to know what is good and what is bad for us. They are not always as reliable as they could be if we have blunted our bodily intelligence through, for example, over-riding signals (such as those that tell us we are over-eating). Signals of fear can also be unreliable; they are too easily set off. And while gut feelings and the like can play a credible reporting role when they relate to what is going on inside of us, the same is not true of external things. As I've said several times, feelings about the numbers that are going to come up in a lottery draw or what the weather is going to be like in a month's time are probably not worth acting upon.

If you don't feel you get feedback sensations from your body, including from your gut and your heart, then maybe it's because you have blunted or lost touch with them. As a rule, the more we operate from our heads, and the more we put our attention on the external world, the more we move away from our internal world and sensitivity to its native intelligence. We certainly had that sensitivity once, when we were babies and toddlers; we cried when we sensed hunger, anxiety or discomfort and gurgled when we sensed that all was well within us. Living a life where we are constantly busy and chronically distracted by the external world, can mean we increasingly lose contact with subtle feedback from within.

Cultivating and learning to tap into the bodily intelligence available to us can significantly benefit our decision-making. Commit to doing that if you feel you currently lack feedback sensations. Your mind-body will provide you with more information than your brain alone. But don't marginalise the brain: listening to your gut alone or acting on a vague intuition might also be unwise.

Being "in touch" with your feelings and bodily sensations as you consider decision-related options is not about being all warm and fuzzy. It's not about having a touchy-feely, New Age or woke sensibility. It's about optimising your chances of guiding your decision-making in the right direction.

Experience tells me that some individuals benefit from having someone else to help them feel and interpret what they are feeling. It can be as simple as "taking them inside" so as to sense what, if anything, they are picking up from, say, their gut. The sensations are sometimes soft and subtle, and only through internal focussing do we even notice them. Also, other people might notice things happening on our outsides—gestures, eye movements, facial expressions etc—that indicate sensations inside of us, ones that we might not be aware of. They can feed these observations back to us and even be us by proxy, as it were, experiencing our sensations vicariously. They tell us what they suspect we might be feeling.

Q8. *A lot of emphasis is usually put upon gathering information in order to make decisions. It doesn't figure heavily in your approach.*

If "information" means facts and figures from the external world then, yes, you are right. I don't talk about it much directly, but hard information does get factored in to most of the decisions I have a hand in. Bits of it can be very useful, and I advise the people I coach to make sure they access it if it's relevant or even vital. For example, lots of big, scary decisions have financial implications even if the central issue isn't about money. So if someone is thinking about leaving their spouse or their job, then it makes sense to look into the financial implications, which might mean seeking information about, say, benefits, voluntary redundancy payments or asset splitting, or about the best way to resource future arrangements.

Someone wrestling with a "Should I, Shouldn't I?" decision about building their own house will need to do a great deal of research into planning and building regulations, consult structural surveyors, architects and probably mortgage brokers and do much more besides. Someone deliberating on whether to have gender reassignment will need to explore the details of the options, the availability and costs of clinical procedures, as well as seeking the "soft" information that counsellors and therapists can provide.

Much the same applies to other decisions with regulatory and technical implication; decisions about whether or not to seek IVF treatment, opt-out of a company pension scheme or declare bankruptcy, for example. For these kinds of decisions, impartial advice from trustworthy experts can be invaluable. In other words, research may be necessary to inform the reasons that people themselves bring to the decision-making table. These often serve as reality checks, indicating whether potential decisions are indeed viable.

But here's the thing: often, the individuals I've worked with are already laden with more "information" in the form of pros and cons than they can cope with. Additional information from the world can be useful in supporting or making them re-think some of their reasons but, pertinent or not, there are situations where it simply won't make any great difference to their final decision. This is especially true of decisions that are primarily matters of personal judgement, requiring more "inside" than "outside" determination.

Significantly, very few of the Killer Questions I've assisted people to formulate, or they have formulated without any direct input from me, have included anything like a hard information component. Killer Questions about leaving (or staying) with partners or employers rarely include the word "money" even if money is relevant. The issue they are wrestling with is often more fundamental, more about personal needs and aspirations, and won't ultimately be determined by "facts". Money and data are more likely to figure in post-decision implementation plans, when the practical steps that follow from a decision come to the fore, such as plans for surviving or thriving when you decide to strike out on your own.

Data mining and analysis can also play a major part in what

I think of as secondary decisions: for example, if the primary decision (settled by the Killer Question) is whether or not to go to university, then the secondary decision is which universities to apply to, and then which offer to accept. (Strictly speaking, that last one is a tertiary decision). There are websites and algorithms to help with decisions like these.

Incidentally, the Killer Question can prove invaluable for secondary decisions as well as initial ones. For many students, the decision of whether or not to apply for a university place is a lot easier than which particular university to go to. The FOTS strategy together with a Killer Question that identifies what is most important to the individual (course appeal? social life? future prospects? etc) will probably be more effective than weighting all the pros and cons of every university in the running.

For me, fact-finding needs to be needs-driven on a case by case basis. It's more germane to some situations than others. It can muddy the waters as well as make them clearer, especially where it serves to deflect an individual from their central issue, bogs them down in nitty-gritty details that are pertinent but not determining or magnifies the significance of a minor consideration.

For example, I once knew a post-retirement couple wrestling with the decision of whether or not to down-size. What held up the decision was the husband's fixation upon matters which to his wife seemed (rightly, I think) trivial in the scheme of things. I don't think he was just finding excuses for staying put; he just couldn't stop focussing upon low-grade cons. I recall the moment when they were on the cusp of committing to a decision; the husband pulled back when he found out about moving costs. His wife was very frustrated.

I've often seen facts skew a decision rather than aid it. Not because of the facts themselves but because of the significance ascribed to them. For example, I've coached a number of well-paid professionals stressed out by their jobs so were contemplating early retirement. What I've encountered frequently is that when they find out what their pension entitlement will be that fact becomes a stumbling block, not because it is inadequate for their needs but because it seems a long way from their current salary. They can't get the two figures, and the discrepancy between them, out of their heads. They are convinced of the decision they should take (retire) but just can't take it. It sometimes takes a period of reconciliation (time to accept the reality of the situation) and/or the right Killer Question for them to un-stick themselves.

Acquiring facts for due diligence purposes is one thing. Allowing them to exert undue influence on the decision, is another. Also, there aren't that many facts about the future. People can be put off making bold but in-their-best-interest decisions by confusing the scenarios in their heads (including imagined "facts") for real ones.

In summary, it's impossible to prescribe how much information should be gathered and the influence it should have on making big, personal decisions. Hard information can be enabling or disabling for the decision-making process. That statement probably runs counter to standard decision-making theory, where research and relevant data gathering is generally regarded as vital early-stage activity. My experience suggests a more nuanced and variable approach is required. It really is an "it all depends" situation.

Q9. You talk about making decisions that are in our "best interests". That makes sense, but is what's in our best interests always obvious?

No, it isn't. The notion of personal "best interests" could take us into great swathes of philosophy, ethics, psychology and other areas besides, so we shall need to keep this simple.

One thing I'm clear about is that some people are more self-aware than others. In this context, it means that they know better what is really in their best interests. I say "really" because it's easy to assume something is in our best interests or a key value for us when it isn't. We've got into the habit of thinking it is, we're deceiving ourselves for some reason or we want to come across as a certain kind of person and this thing is associated with this kind of person. So, for example, I might say to myself and others that being community minded is important to me when really it's not that important, or that having a highly paid but demanding job is in my best interests when that's not really the case.

In particular, it's very possible to identify something that matters to you but believe it matters more (or less) than it really does. I'm sure this is one reason that people have trouble with the balance approach. They can't accurately assign a weight to some of the pros and cons because they don't really know how important they are. I've worked with people who say they care about working in teams or getting praise from their bosses or spending time with their children but actually don't care about these things too much. For example, I once worked with a man who said how much he cared about being with his son. When I pointed out to him, after we'd done a time audit of his life, that he actually spent twice as long at the gym than he did with his son, he was shocked: initially defensive but later saddened by the truth that one-to-one time with his son was probably not a priority. This learning point was highly pertinent to the decision he had to make.

When someone asks me to assist them to think through a big decision, I need to put their personal best interests centre-stage. I will encourage them to work out and question what those best interests are. I will also encourage them, if they should need it, which most people don't, to consider the interests of those who might be affected by their decisions. Very often this includes partners and children or work colleagues, sometimes other family members, neighbours and other groups of people. Sometimes what is in the best interests of the person concerned is also in the best interests of affected parties.

It was in the case of the businessman I mentioned earlier whose wife and children agreed that his retraining as a teacher would benefit them all. Sometimes it's seemingly not, as when someone decides to leave a partner who doesn't want them to leave. But reality is complex, and it may actually turn out to be more in their interests than they think at the time. As I've made plain, there's often a difference between short-term interests and long-term ones, and that a common failure is to make decisions that avoid immediate discomfort but are inimical to long-term interests.

I've also made it clear, I hope, that every decision has to be made at a particular point in time and with a particular time horizon in view. From one point in time we may interpret our best interests very differently from another point. "Wisdom in hindsight" is an example of this phenomenon.

One thing I am clear about is that our "best interests" should be seen in the round, as comprehensively as possible, because then we can make an holistic judgement. The truth is, a decision we make can be both for and against our best interests at the same time. On several occasions, for example, I have worked with individuals whose big, scary decisions were about whether or not they should speak out about something they knew was wrong and they also knew would have negative consequences for them if they did speak out. It's the decision-making quandary of whistle-blowers.

The best interests of these individuals was not straightforward. It was not in their best interests job-wise and career-wise. For some of them, they also knew that speaking out would end friendships and make them targets of vilification. On the other hand, they knew it was not in their best interests to say nothing. To do so would ruin their peace of mind and make it hard to "live with themselves".

Sometimes in deciding what counts as best interests, or to which best interests to give priority, tough judgements have to be made.

So deciding "best interests" can be challenging and is certainly not just about (or even about) "what will make me most happy". Enlisting the assistance of the whole of the body's intelligence can be key, as is thinking through the situation in as wide-ranging way as necessary. The term "best interests" might suggest a narrow focus upon the individual (what I call a "worm's-eye perspective") but it's usually better arrived at through a combination of that and a "bird's-eye" (i.e. big picture) perspective. Used in a complementary way, these are likely to enable as wise a decision as possible.

Q.10 The book is clearly focussed mainly on the big and challenging decisions that individuals, couples and families or similar small groups have to make. You say something about public sphere decision-making, but are the strategies you suggest as applicable to communities and organisations such as companies and even governments?

Some of them certainly are. Obviously, big "public" decisions such as those about policies, major infrastructure projects and development strategies are multi-factorial and very complex. They require a lot of research, data gathering and analysis, and often need to take account of the views of many people and organisations. Nowadays, technology is likely to play a major part. This can range from mathematical modelling, the application of advanced statistical techniques and computer algorithms to social media surveys and even public enquiries. Account might be taken (it nearly always should be) of emotional and psychological factors, such as how people feel about possible decisions and its impact on their wellbeing, as well as upon the wellbeing of communities and the environment. What we might call the ecosystemic context for decision-making is always likely to be more complex for decisions in the public sphere and the requirements for explanation and transparency greater.

Having said all that, the fundamental prescriptions I proffer—be aware of the inherent problems of a balance (pros and cons) approach, favour diagnostic approaches, including the use of tests and tick-box conditions, and the elimination of the relatively inconsequential in order to focus upon the most consequential factors, are relevant to all decision-making situations. So, above all, is the use of the Killer Question. However massive the whole consultation/deliberation/decision-making process might be, the decision in the end usually boils down to something quite stark and simple;

for example, to build or not to build. So yes, I modestly suggest that the Killer Question could be as valuable for making the biggest decisions as for making the smallest. When it comes down to it, a decision is a decision.

Notes

1 **Notes From a Friend,** Anthony Robbins (Simon & Schuster, 1996)

2 I'm not the first person to refer to the pros and cons approach to making decisions as the balance approach, but I have been doing so for more than a quarter of a century. The same with the diagnostic approach to which I contrast it. I've recently become aware that these two methods figure prominently in an excellent book on making decisions in the context of relationships: **Too Good to Leave, Too Bad to Stay** by Mira Kirshenbaum (Dutton 1996). It's a book I recommend.

3 You can do no better than spend time on HeartMath Institute website if you want to explore the evidence that the heart and brain work in tandem. Neuro-cardiology is a field of clinical science, but some within the field also focus on its impact on our bodily intelligence, intuitions and how the heart's "brain" interacts with the brain itself. There is now a huge body of literature on the gut and its importance, including as a source of guidance and wisdom. You'll find lots of very accessible pieces on-line: for example, "How Your Gut Instinct Works" (https://www.huffingtonpost.co.uk/becky-walsh/how-your-gut-instinct-wor_b_4765467.html), "5 Gut Instincts You Shouldn't Ignore" by Courtney Helgoe (https://experiencelife.lifetime.life/article/5-gut-instincts-you-shouldnt-ignore/) and "3 Reasons Why You Have to Trust Your Gut" by Susanna Newsonen (https://www.psychologytoday.com/us/blog/the-path-passionate-happiness/201505/3-reasons-why-you-have-trust-your-gut).

Other books by the author

Becoming Guise-Wise: how we can make one simple change in us to end conflict and division and take our species to another level
(Olympia Publishers, 2022)
www.commonality-first.com

The Power of Surge: achieving big things quickly for you, your team, your community, your organisation… and the world
(Olympia Publishers, 2020)
www.surgestudies.org

Stopping bad things happening to good schools and good school leaders
(John Catt Educational Limited, 2018)

The Element Dictionary of Personal Development: an A-Z of the Most Widely-Used Terms, Theories and Concepts
(Element, 1996)

The Garden in Victorian Literature
(Scolar Press, 1988)

Printed in Great Britain
by Amazon

33014130R00106